Doing Film Studies

D1342786

Doing Film Studies examines what it really means to study film, encouraging the reader to question the dominant theories as well as understanding the key approaches to cinema. This book provides an overview of the construction of film studies – including its history and evolution – and examines the application of theories to film texts. Important questions discussed include:

- Why does film studies need a canon?
- What is the relationship between authorship and genre theory?
- What is screen theory?
- How do we read a film text?
- Why is the concept of the spectator important to film?
- How is film involved in national identity?
- What is meant by a 'film industry'?

Aimed at students in their final year of secondary education or beginning their degrees, *Doing Film Studies* equips the reader with the tools needed in approaching the study of film.

Sarah Casey Benyahia is a teacher of Film and Media Studies. She is the author of *Crime* (2011) and *Teaching Contemporary British Cinema* (2005), and co-author of several film and media studies text books.

Claire Mortimer is a teacher of Media and Film Studies. She is the author of *Romantic Comedy* (2010) and co-author of *AS Media Studies: The Essential Introduction for WJEC* (2011).

Also Available from Routledge

Cinema Studies: The Key Concepts
Susan Hayward
978-0-415-36782-0

Film Studies: The Basics
Amy Villarejo
978-0-415-36139-2

Film: The Essential Study Guide
Edited by Ruth Doughty and Deborah Shaw
978-0-415-43700-4

Doing Film Studies

A Subject Guide for Students

*Sarah Casey Benyahia
and Claire Mortimer*

Routledge
Taylor & Francis Group

LONDON AND NEW YORK

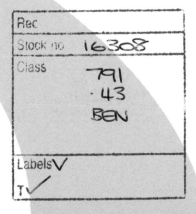

First published 2013
by Routledge
2 Park Square, Milton Park, Abingdon, Oxon OX14 4RN

Simultaneously published in the USA and Canada
by Routledge
711 Third Avenue, New York, NY 10017

*Routledge is an imprint of the Taylor & Francis Group,
an informa business*

British Library Cataloguing in Publication Data
A catalogue record for this book is available from the British Library

Library of Congress Cataloging in Publication Data
Benyahia, Sarah Casey.
Doing film studies : a subject guide for students / Sarah Casey
Benyahia and Claire Mortimer.
p. cm.
Includes bibliographical references and index.
1. Motion pictures.   I. Mortimer, Claire, 1964-   II. Title.
PN1994.B4337 2012
791.43 – dc23

                                   2012020499

ISBN: 978-0-415-60269-3 (hbk)
ISBN: 978-0-415-60270-9 (pbk)
ISBN: 978-0-203-08086-3 (ebk)

Typeset in Times NRMT
by RefineCatch Limited, Bungay, Suffolk

Printed and bound in Great Britain by
TJ International Ltd, Padstow, Cornwall

Contents

Acknowledgements

The authors are very grateful to Andy Humphries, their editor at Routledge, for his constructive and good humoured guidance throughout this project.

Claire would like to thank Granville, Arthur and Flo, as always.

Sarah would like to thank her mother for her continued interest and encouragement.

Introduction

About this Book

What does it mean to be 'doing film studies'?

The experience of studying film is diverse, covering a range of academic levels as well as theoretical and practical approaches. You may be doing film studies as an A level or IB student, or have begun an undergraduate – even postgraduate – course in film. Whatever stage you are at, this book aims to give an understanding of the evolution of the subject and to get you to think analytically about why we study film in the way we do. *Doing Film Studies* does have aspects of a conventional textbook – it includes an overview of the key theories and thinkers in the discipline – but can also be thought of as a 'meta' textbook, one which explains why film studies takes the form it does. For example, in addition to explaining what the auteur theory is and illustrating how it can be used to analyse films, we are equally interested in asking why this theory became so prominent in film studies and what prompted later arguments against it. Therefore, this is a book which asks *why* we study particular types of films and not others (which you may think are equally worthy of study), and *why* we use the particular approaches that we do.

As a student of film studies, it is important to understand the background of this relatively young subject, to consider how it became possible to study film. Many of the competing claims of the different theoretical approaches and methodologies come from the discipline's need to establish itself as a subject that should be taken seriously, an obstacle that has faced all attempts to study forms of popular culture. The development of the discipline itself forms the framework of this book, looking at the very first attempts to 'do film studies' at the beginning of the twentieth century and considering how the early definition of film as an art form belonging to high, not popular, culture has shaped later developments.

How to use this book

The book is divided into four sections.

Part I: What we watch and what we study

This introductory section takes as its starting point the make-up of film studies courses today, examining the film syllabus for A level and undergraduate courses and asking why we study what we study – what are the shared characteristics of contemporary film studies courses? This analysis provides the backdrop for the book's investigation into how film studies has developed to this point.

Part II: The history of film studies

This section addresses how the study of film became institutionalized as an academic subject, tracing its development from the work of film fans and enthusiasts (the role of 'cinephilia') to the emergence of film theory, the highly specialized range of approaches that reinforced film studies' position as a university subject. Part II provides a historical overview of the subject in the UK and US, as well as considering the function of the canon and the key theoretical approaches of the subject – auteur theory and genre studies.

Part III: Studying the film text

As will soon become apparent, one of the central concerns in debates about how film should be studied was the fear that theoretical approaches were in danger of losing sight of the film itself, particularly the way in which the language of film constructed meaning. This section examines the ways in which films have been 'read' through the emphasis on textual analysis and narratology, and the way in which the interpretive relationship between the film and the spectator has been conceived.

Part IV: Film as a contemporary discipline

Part IV examines the current experience of 'doing film studies' through reference to some recent developments and changes of emphasis in the curriculum. These include the focus on film and identity, and historical approaches to the film industry. It is through recent developments in the discipline that the influence of other related subject areas such as media and cultural studies are apparent, and which may suggest the future nature of 'doing film studies'.

Each chapter is introduced with an overview of the key questions to be addressed and concludes with a summary of the ideas discussed. At the end of each chapter is a list of the authors and works referred to, as well as some suggestions for further reading which will help you to research the area in greater depth.

Further reading

There are many excellent film textbooks which provide comprehensive discussions of film theories from a range of different approaches, several of which we refer to in the course of this book.

The following may be useful in informing your studies:

Cook, P. (ed) (2008) *The Cinema Book*, 3rd edition, British Film Institute, London
Dix, A. (2008) *Beginning Film Studies*, Manchester University Press, Manchester
Hill, J. and Church Gibson, P. (eds) (1998) *The Oxford Guide to Film Studies*, Oxford University Press, Oxford
Maltby, R. (2003) *Hollywood Cinema*, 2nd edition, Blackwell, London
Turner, G. (1998) *Film as Social Practice*, Routledge, London

A useful guide to film theory where the key debates are discussed in detail is *Approaches to Popular Film*, edited by Joanne Hollows and Mark Jancovich (Manchester University Press, 1995).

A very readable guide to the history of film (and the basis for a subsequent television series) is Mark Cousins's *The Story of Film* (Pavilion, 2004).

Finally, a handy guide to key terms and theories is Susan Hayward's *Cinema Studies: The Key Concepts* (Routledge, 2000).

PART I

WHAT WE WATCH AND WHAT WE STUDY

1

The Canon in Practice

In having chosen to undertake the study of film, you will have quickly become aware of how popular the subject now is in higher education, being widely on offer in a range of institutions, in a bewildering variety of permutations. It may be difficult to imagine how the subject had to struggle to be accepted by academia, meeting with initial suspicion and disdain, perhaps because of the obvious associations with popular culture and mass entertainment, seemingly at odds with serious academic study. This debate around the popular and the academic is central to understanding the nature of film studies.

Before engaging with how film has become the subject that it is today, we need to consider what exactly is involved in studying it: what is the typical course content? What films will you be expected to study and why study those films, in particular? What can you expect to learn from them?

As with any academic subject, what constitutes film studies has been shaped by a variety of forces and influential figures over time to form the subject you experience today. Film itself is a comparatively young form and has only been in existence since the late nineteenth century. It is also a relatively young subject, having gained academic credibility in the last 30 years after fighting for acceptance. The form in which we find it today reflects the values and input of significant 'players' in the academic world, but also reflects a subject which is itself in flux. The technology of film-making, distribution and exhibition itself has undergone massive changes in a very short space of time with the impact of digital technologies.

A typical film studies degree will offer a grounding in film history and film theory, developing critical and analytical skills, with a core emphasis on Hollywood cinema. Beyond this a course will offer opportunities to explore other aspects of film, such as national cinemas, specific directors, specific film movements (for example, the French New Wave or film noir), film genres and critical issues (such as gender and film). Some courses will also offer creative opportunities such as practical film-making and screenwriting.

The popular experience of film bears little connection to the academic film landscape in terms of the films which feature in the film curriculum, and which are critically rated by the film cognoscenti. Film is primarily an industry, being a significant aspect of popular culture, where everyone has their own concepts of their personal film greats. Unlike literature, theatre and other arts, film is a popular art form and thus is universally 'owned' by the populace; everyone has an opinion as to what makes a good film. During recent years there has been a growing academic recognition of the importance of popular culture, as is evident in influential research such as Henry Jenkins's seminal work on fandom.

Film studies today is derived from a blend of approaches and theory from a range of different disciplines, including anthropology, art, theatre, literature and linguistics, which have informed the critical and theoretical approaches to the subject. The landscape of the subject is mapped out around the film canon – that is, a core of 'classic' films which are understood to have been vital in the development of the form, and which are seen to define the 'best' of film in all its key phases to date. In this respect the canon is the core of the subject, the filmic equivalent of Chaucer, Shakespeare, Austen et al. The canon has always been crucial to academics in staking their claim that film is an art form, epitomized by certain essential texts, which signpost a critical history of 'great' moments: great films, directors or film movements.

What we watch

The universal experience of cinema for most students is dominated by popular Hollywood cinema. The exploration of *why* this is the case forms a key area of study, involving a consideration of film history and debates touching on global politics, economic forces and cultural hegemony. The popularity of Hollywood cinema is reflected in box office statistics.

The box office is dominated by films funded by the major Hollywood film studios, many of which gain global success, beyond the English-speaking market, and thus dominate world cinemas, indicating the continuing power of popular Hollywood film. For example, the highest grossing films in the UK in 2010 reveal certain trends, such as the popularity of fantasy, whether it be animation (*Toy Story 3*), the superhero genre (*Iron Man 2*), sci-fi (*Inception*) or vampire romance (*The Twilight Saga: Eclipse*). Many of the highest grossing films prove Hollywood's success in targeting the family market, but also demonstrate how Hollywood continues to be risk-averse, with a reliance on sequels, and adaptations of narratives which have already been successful, as books, television series or cartoon characters for example. It is also helpful to consider what is missing. The ten highest grossing films at the UK box office featured no films produced by a UK studio, only *Harry Potter and the Deathly Hallows (Part One)* has any claim to being a British film. The absolute majority of the films are set in the US and there are no British directors featured in the list.

What do we learn from these lists?

In this context, 'popular' cinema is the cinema that is most widely consumed – this can be crassly measured by box office receipts. In most cases these will be the films that are produced by the few dominant Hollywood studios, owned by the vast media conglomerates that have a global presence. Nevertheless, these are generally not the films that gain critical esteem and academic kudos, and will not form the core of any film studies degree course.

There is clearly a substantial gap between the cinema which is part of popular consciousness, and the cinema that informs the world of academia. This is clear when comparing the top ten box office hits of 2010 with the critics' top films of the year as chosen by *Sight and Sound* magazine. There is no common ground between the two, the top five films of the year, according to the critics, being:

1 *The Social Network* (David Fincher), US;
2 *Uncle Boonmee Who Can Recall His Past Lives* (*Lung Boonmee raluek chat*), Thailand/UK/France/Germany/Spain/The Netherlands/US;
3 *Another Year* (Mike Leigh), UK;
4 *Carlos* (Olivier Assayas), France/Germany/Belgium;
5 *The Arbor* (Clio Barnard), UK.

Sight and Sound is the monthly magazine produced by the British Film Institute (BFI), whose remit is to promote 'understanding and appreciation of film and television heritage and culture'. This emphasis on education and enlightenment is reflected in its 'best' films of the year, a list which is notable for prioritizing films which would not be easy to find in the multiplex (with the exception of *The Social Network*) and, consequently, offer a different experience of cinema from the mainstream. These films are largely made by independent studios, on smaller budgets, relying less on stars and special effects for their appeal, and they reflect the output of national cinemas away from the Hollywood juggernaut.

Sight and Sound creates a different landscape for the appreciation of what is 'great' and of value when considering cinema. Its choices reflect an appreciation of film as art and as the product of an artist, rather than offering the seemingly ephemeral pleasures of the cinema of the multiplex. The ultimate list of 'greatness' in film is the critics' top ten film list produced by *Sight and Sound* magazine every ten years, purporting to be a list of the best films of all time. The first poll was held in 1952, as the movement towards a more serious approach to film appreciation gathered momentum. For many commentators and academics, this list defines the film canon, subsequently having immense influence and, in turn, reflecting the defining currents in the world of film studies.

The 2012 critics' poll top ten is as follows:

1. *Vertigo* (Hitchcock, 1958)
2. *Citizen Kane* (Welles, 1941)
3. *Tokyo Story* (Ozu, 1953)
4. *La Règle du Jeu* (Renoir, 1939)
5. *Sunrise: A Song of Two Humans* (Murnau, 1927)
6. *2001: A Space Odyssey* (Kubrick, 1968)
7. *The Searchers* (Ford, 1956)
8. *Man With a Movie Camera* (Vertov, 1929)
9. *The Passion of Joan of Arc* (Dreyer, 1927)
10. *8½* (Fellini, 1963)

(*Sight and Sound*, September 2012)

Such a list maps out a charter for the study of film, clearly signposting the film 'greats' by an esteemed body of opinion. It forms an agenda for the history of film, which sees the most significant films having been produced in a 40-year span between the late silent era and the auteurist American cinema of the 1960s. Another notable aspect of this list is a history of film which hinges on the work of auteurs – a view of cinema which sees it as the work of artists and, thus, staking its claim as an art form, rather than merely a form of popular culture.

The educational remit of the British Film Institute informs its programme of events, structured around screenings and seasons celebrating key figures and important cinemas. The programme for 2011 features seasons celebrating the work of Elizabeth Taylor and Dirk Bogart in addition to a Soviet science fiction festival and a retrospective of films from the Art Theatre Guild of Japan. Likewise, the American Film Institute (AFI) and the Canadian Film Institute (CFI) hold a similar remit in undertaking a key role in contributing to film education and as cultural archivists for their national cinemas.

The work of the AFI and the BFI is clearly reflected in the curriculum for the teaching of film studies, effectively establishing a roster of films which are worthy of study and staking out the critical areas of interest regarding the history of film. The wider debate as to what should be studied is reflected in the curriculum, as can be seen in the list of films to choose from for close critical study in the 2010 specification for WJEC's A-level Film Studies course:

- *Modern Times* (Chaplin, 1936), US;
- *Les Enfants du Paradis* (Carné, 1945), France;
- *Vertigo* (Hitchcock, 1958), US;
- *The Battle of Algiers* (Pontecorvo, 1966), Algeria/Italy;
- *Sweet Sweetback's Baadasssss Song* (Van Peebles, 1971), US;
- *Solaris* (Tarkovsky, 1972), USSR;
- *Happy Together* (Wong Kar Wai, 1997), Hong Kong;
- *Fight Club* (Fincher, 1999), US;
- *Talk to Her* (Almodovar, 2002), Spain;
- *Morvern Callar* (Ramsay, 2002), UK.

The list features four US films; yet, in the spirit of the specification, each raises debates in terms of how they challenge the Hollywood mainstream. The other films represent a range of national cinemas, genres and points in film history. It is notable that the films can be deemed to be the work of auteurs, in the spirit of the key arbiters of critical taste such as *Sight and Sound*.

What makes a great film?

Dean Simonton, professor of psychology at UC Davis, has undertaken scientific research into the issue of what makes a 'great flick', publishing the results in his book *Great Flicks: Scientific Studies of Cinematic Creativity and Aesthetics* (Oxford University Press, 2011):

> A film that wins critical acclaim is likely to be an R-rated drama, adapted from a prize-winning play or book and based on a true story, with the original author or director involved in writing the screenplay. It is unlikely to be a sequel or remake, a comedy or musical, a summer release, a big-budget project, have a PG-13 rating, open on numerous screens or do a big box office on the first weekend. It probably has an excellent score, but it may not have an award-winning song. But box-office hits may have entirely different profiles.
>
> http://www.sciencedaily.com/releases/2007/08/070815135034.htm

This broad summary of his research touches on the intrinsic chasm between what qualifies as greatness in terms of critical response and the films which actually prosper at the box office. Nevertheless, such a cursory survey of the industrial context is noteworthy in terms of revealing certain superficial factors which seem to differentiate between popular and critical success.

A closer examination of the *Sight and Sound* poll reveals more about the critical landscape which informs the film curriculum. The top-ranked film in the critics' poll is *Vertigo*, having replaced *Citizen Kane* which had occupied the top spot for half a century. The accompanying comments praise *Vertigo* for being 'pure cinema', with 'its pictorial splendour' and 'delirious excess' (Matthews 2012: 54–5). The film is described as 'yield[ing] an intense, surrealist poetry' with the power to 'illuminate the inner "moral value" of things'. Technical virtuosity and stylistic verve are key factors in the selection of the films, alongside the celebration of films that stake out new territory in terms of their message and narrative. For example, *La Règle du Jeu* is praised for being an 'unsparing depiction of French life in 1939' (Bell 2012: 51). The films are largely discussed in terms of an auteurist agenda, specifically as to how they manifest the signature of the director, although occasionally commenting on other creative contributions, such as soundtrack and cinematography.

Summary

- The academic approach to film is structured around a wider consensus about what makes a film worthy of study, based upon ideas about greatness.

- The canon provides insights into cinema beyond Hollywood, as well as directing us to defining texts in the history of cinema.
- The curriculum for film is constantly developing, moving increasingly towards recognition of the importance of studying the popular alongside the 'great'.
- The study of what we watch needs to embrace the wider historical and stylistic context of film.

References

Bell, J. (2012) 'La Régle du Jeu', *Sight and Sound*, September: p51.
Matthews, P. (2012) 'Vertigo', *Sight and Sound*, September: pp54–5.

PART II

THE HISTORY OF
FILM STUDIES

The History of the Discipline, or How It Became Possible to Study Film

In this chapter we will consider:

- the aims behind the first film studies courses;
- the development from film appreciation and cinephilia to film theory;
- the obstacles facing an academic discipline where the focus is on popular culture;
- the importance of authorship theory in enabling film studies to become an academic discipline.

Film studies is a young subject. This simple phrase needs clarifying. It is young in comparison with science, which can claim a history of thousands of years; perhaps surprisingly, however, it is not much newer than English, which has been taught and studied since the beginning of the twentieth century. It is older than media studies, with which it shares some content and approaches. The descriptive title itself – film studies – has not always been in use; courses on the study of film have, for example, been entitled 'film appreciation', 'cinema studies' or 'screen studies' at different periods and in different places. During recent years, the development of cultural studies courses has further complicated the use of titles for courses which study film. Film studies degrees are theoretical courses but may include a greater or lesser amount of practical production work, blurring the line between these and more technical or vocational courses.

These complications are part of the wider debate over what constitutes a subject or discipline. It may be the case that defining film studies as a discipline is more difficult than defining English or history; but all disciplinary areas share a process of debate and competing claims for what should and should not be included in that discipline. In this case, it is also a debate about whether film should even be studied as an academic discipline.

This chapter will show how it became possible to be 'doing film', beginning with the early attempts to teach film, a consideration of the aims in teaching about film and the obstacles in the way of developing this practice. The history of the development of the discipline of film studies is illuminating not just in the specifics of this subject, but also because film studies encompasses many of the fundamental debates around education: what should be studied? Who should be educated? What is the purpose of education? To all of these questions could be added a secondary question: who decides? Defining film studies as a discipline has also involved the separation of popular commercial writing about film from academic research in universities. All of these areas are addressed in the first developments in the subject, in the very earliest attempts to study film.

Why should film be studied: The aims of 'doing film'

The ideology underpinning the first studies of film was the desire to educate the audience and to control a new form of entertainment. The first courses in the US and the UK to take film as a focus of study were guided by the idea of 'moral uplift'. As a relatively new medium with a mass working-class audience, cinema was treated with some fear and anxiety by political, religious and educational groups. Their concern was about the effects that watching films in dark auditoriums might have, particularly when the quality of the films in terms of storylines, performances and production values was deemed to be low.

The first attempts to study film in a systematic, coherent way were characterized by contradictions and division, which are still apparent in contemporary debates about the nature of doing film. This is, in part, a consequence of the particular character of film as both an art form and a business, as a field which lent itself to vocational and academic practices, but also as a new medium which provoked anxiety about its effects. These early approaches included:

- film appreciation, where good films were a form of 'moral uplift';
- film as ideology, transmitting messages to society;
- instruction on how to run a business (the film industry);

- teaching technical skills such as scriptwriting;
- psycho-social effects of film: what was the relationship between films and human behaviour?

In practice, the pedagogical impetus behind the first courses tended to have a combination of these different approaches, indicating the interdisciplinary nature of the subject; but at this stage it was very unusual for the early study of film to focus exclusively on the concept of film as art. The historiography of film studies as a discipline is itself a developing area. Recent research has demonstrated that film was the subject of study much earlier than previously understood; the first courses appeared in US universities as early as the first decade of the twentieth century. This revisionism of the history of doing film is, in part, to do with how the beginning of a discipline is defined. Earlier histories of film studies had defined the beginning of the subject as the institutionalization of film studies in universities. This is a definition which characterizes a discipline as existing only when a body of research has been produced by academics in universities, has been published in specialist journals and passed on to postgraduate students. This meant that film studies could be dated only from the 1950s when academic frameworks such as auteur theory were first developed. Polan (2007) demonstrates that this is only a partial account of the history of the discipline based on a problematic definition, one which ignores the teaching of the subject in classrooms; 'practical efforts of day to day pedagogy generally are played down in the historiography of disciplines' (Polan, 2007, p20). In *Scenes of Instruction*, Polan argues that the conventional history of the teaching of film has constructed a heroic narrative where film academics battled against a closed system of old-fashioned university departments in a similar manner to the auteur directors battling against the studio system. Instead, Polan shows that the first courses on film at US universities existed from 1915 onwards. This selection of courses from 1915 to 1935 do not constitute a coherent set of practices which characterize the traditional definition of an academic discipline, but do reflect the fact that film was seen by some teachers and curriculum directors at US universities as 'a specific, definable and teachable subject of academic intention'. The teachers of these courses were dealing with questions recognizable to contemporary film teachers about the nature of studying film: how to combine the critical study of film with the practical aspect, how to develop a way of analysing the aesthetics of cinema, how to reconcile the relationship between film and other art forms. In addition, there was the question of compatibility: could film be studied as both an art form and a business? Didn't the one contradict the other? There was also the fundamental question of what the focus of study should be: should Hollywood cinema dominate?

The obstacles to constructing the discipline of film studies were various. The overlap with other subjects, particularly literature, meant that it was often studied as another way of telling stories rather than as a specific form in itself. The struggle for film studies has been to define the discipline as separate from literature (and other subjects), but simultaneously to acknowledge the fact that film as a subject is interdisciplinary by its nature. The first film courses in the US were housed in departments of literature, history, social sciences and business schools. With the development of new academic subjects in the 1980s and 1990s, film courses were often subsumed into media and communications or cultural studies where the specificity of film was again lost.

The ubiquity of film across courses was (and, to an extent, still is) a further problem in the construction of film studies as a discipline. It is used in a variety of different ways in the wider curriculum, but usually as a carrier for something else. This might be to illustrate historical events, show an adaptation of a Shakespeare play, as an aid to the study of foreign languages, or in its traditional, educational documentary role. This variety of functions, along with the common assumption that the watching of a film provides light relief in a more important, serious subject, has contributed to the difficulty of outlining the boundary of film studies as a discipline. It is part of the same obstacle to study which assumes that because everyone (including a baby) can watch a film, there cannot be anything to study or learn.

The combination of art and commerce, which is the focus of film studies in a way that is not true of other subjects, also had a negative impact upon the development of the discipline. A discipline has to be a subject deemed worthy of study and exactly what constitutes this worth changes over time. As a film studies student, you are probably very well aware that the subject has been seen as a 'soft option' or even a 'Mickey Mouse' degree by people who don't really understand what film studies is. Just as in previous generations English and sociology – and, currently, media studies – were decried for their lack of academic rigour, film studies has been on the receiving end of a great deal of uninformed attack, often based on the idea that studying film must be easy because watching films is pleasurable and a form of mass entertainment.

In the UK, the first impulses to take film seriously as a focus of study were provoked by concerns about the relationship between the young audience and cinema; it was in schools rather than universities that the first film teaching took place. This developed in the context of a broader debate about the effects of the emerging popular culture. These debates in the 1930s were dominated by groups other than teachers, with politicians, religious leaders and the press having the most influence on the discussion of the role of film in public life. From this perspective film education is much more to do with social policy than with the study of an art form. It did, though, provide the impetus for the setting up of the British Film Institute (BFI), which in turn became the most influential provider of film education in the UK, both in terms of supporting teacher training from the 1930s onwards and through its education department, developing what became known as film theory.

In 1933, the British government commissioned a report entitled *The Film in National Life*, which examined the way in which film could be used educationally and culturally to shape the taste of the audience, to educate them in how to watch and what to watch. In turn, it was believed that this would affect the type of films being produced by the industry. If the audience was educated to understand what were good and bad films, then in the future it would only make economic sense to make 'good' films. These ideas indicate the key concerns and impulses around the early teaching and study of film: the desire to define the difference between good and bad films, the belief that film could have a negative effect on its audience, and the conception that film is a vehicle for education rather than an object of study itself.

During the 1930s and 1940s there was a clear attempt to create hierarchical categories of films between those which had educational value and those which were merely for entertainment. This division was reinforced through the separation of documentary and commercial (rather than fiction) cinema. Documentary film was seen as a vehicle to educate the audience within the classroom and the cinema itself, whereas the entertainment or commercial film could not be used for education as it lacked 'moral uplift'. What defines the educational or teaching film at this period can be understood from the lists of films for study drawn up by bodies such as the BFI and film appreciation societies. These would provide the first attempt at producing a canon in the teaching of film. Many of these judgements about acceptable and non-acceptable films are based on concerns (in the UK) about the Americanization of the culture, as well as the tone of commercial film. Popular forms of cinema such as slapstick and melodrama were deemed to be entertainment associated with a young audience and without instructional value. 'Bad' taste is defined as childlike; part of the aim of educating the cinema audience was to move them away from what were deemed simple, immature pleasures to more sophisticated adult tastes. In an approach which is still apparent in the curriculum of film courses today, early film pedagogues believed that they had to meet their pupils on their level of taste in film before moving on to the more difficult but rewarding pleasures of instructional film. In this attitude to good and bad taste, film educators were typical of their time; but it is clear that debates about which films were worthy of attention soon made this a much more complex and subtle analysis.

School film appreciation and film societies

The BFI was instrumental in training and encouraging the development of film education through their work with film appreciation societies during the 1940s and 1950s, particularly those set up in schools and as part of adult education centres. The BFI ran a summer school for teachers interested in the teaching of film as early as the 1930s, and these continued up until the 1970s. Film teaching was not part of the curriculum at this period (the first assessed course was in 1972) and tended to be taught through after-school film appreciation societies. Many teachers involved argued that it was important to teach film within the school timetable. This was a way of raising its status but also a response to financial constraints; after-school film societies relied on subscription fees from the students for funding. However, there were arguments for the retention of film appreciation outside of the official curriculum. In a BFI report on film societies, one school teacher argued that 'the great value of the film society lies in its ability to cater for large audiences drawn from practically the whole school. Children growing up through the school will then see a considerable number of worthwhile films and come to think and talk about them in a critical way' (Hodgkinson et al, 1950).

The pedagogical aims of the societies are apparent in the discussion of the appropriate age for pupils to begin film appreciation. It is clear that the idea of training taste and the concept of moral uplift are important. In considering the right age to begin film education, a distinction is made between teaching the 'tricks of the trade' – the technical components of film – and film criticism. The first could be discussed from an age of 10 years while the latter demanded a greater degree of intelligence and maturity; the average age for this was seen as 13 or 14. This is reiterated in the evaluation of the effects of frequent cinema going outside of the film society programme. Many teachers did argue that it was helpful, with the keenest cinema-goers also the most enthusiastic members of the societies. It was also felt, though, that pupils who went to the cinema frequently needed to be educated about film earlier; there was a concern that these 'film fans' were in danger of already losing their 'freshness of taste'. The discussion of age therefore was not only motivated by a child's ability to comprehend, but by a sense that the programme must be studied as early as possible in order to prevent the development of bad habits in terms of taste in film; 'a compromise must be made between the development of the critical facilities and the danger of the early development of an undiscriminating cinema-going habit' (Hodgkinson et al, 1950). This was seen as particularly important for state school children because it was argued that pupils at boarding school didn't go to the cinema as often, although it is likely that there was also a concern that working-class children were more vulnerable to the influence of cinema.

The practice of early film education in the UK can be characterized as a form of cinephilia; the passionate embracing of the details of a subject associated with 'amateurs' rather than academics linked to an institution. Cinephilia plays an important role in the development of film studies as a way of spreading enthusiasm and knowledge, but also in developing the first materials for the study of film in the form of film societies, programme notes, discussion groups and the writing of reviews. The later development of the academic discipline meant a shift away, and in some accounts a definitive break, from the concerns of cinephilia, which were seen as fact-driven detail, to the move towards a theory of film.

The first film courses in the US were characterized as instructional and practical rather than academic. This was because film could not be conceived of as an art form as it differed fundamentally from traditional definitions of what art is. Film was a collaborative, technical and reproducible medium made in factories to produce a profit from distribution to a mass audience. Films were not viewed in silent contemplation and then re-examined and studied but were consumed by a loud, often uneducated, active audience. Once watched there was not the easy possibility of viewing them again – something which didn't change dramatically until the introduction of video tapes in the 1980s. This made the study of film in the past fundamentally different than our own recent experience, where films are available for immediate re-watching and checking; no need to try and memorize shots and dialogue! There was no archive or museum of cinema, and therefore no history to provide context and evaluation for the study of film. All of these elements were in direct contradiction to definitions of art at the beginning of the twentieth century. Art was the creation of an individual who was divinely gifted and superior to his or her peers; it was beneficial and good for the soul; it could only be truly appreciated by educated elite, but the effects of great art, carefully defined by dominant groups, could trickle down to the wider parts of the population.

The development and influence of auteur theory

The divide between film and high culture led to a fundamental debate about how film should be studied; whether the aspects which define it as different from high art should be acknowledged or whether the definitions of high art, including its function as a form of moral instruction, should be moulded onto film, enabling it to be defined as an art form and therefore worthy of study. The terms of this debate were central to the development of auteur theory in the 1950s. Auteur theory was fundamental to the development of film studies as a discipline and remained dominant in film courses until the 1980s.

Auteur theory in film studies is based on the idea that an individual is the source of meaning and value in artistic texts. This is an old, well-established idea in the arts and goes back to the Renaissance when the idea of the uniquely, divinely gifted artist emerged, where the individual was seen as the sole creator of their work (e.g. Michelangelo's 'David', Leonardo's 'Mona Lisa'). Before that artists were artisans, respected manual workers who belonged to guilds or unions and were valued for their practical, decorative abilities. This new concept of the artist developed into a Romantic ideal, based on the idea of a misunderstood genius struggling against the conventions of society to achieve their vision. This 'true artist' was separated from the wider social or political context, able to transcend their specific place and time. This idea of the embattled, often unrecognized genius is a familiar representation of the artist in films, from Vincent van Gogh (*Lust for Life,* 1956) to Jackson Pollock (*Pollock*, 2000). It is an image which seems to fit easily into a wider conception of the artist as more driven, more talented, but more tortured than the rest of us. The concept of the individual artist as the creator of the work of art is relatively easy to apply to traditional arts such as painting and literature (although even here the notion of the artist as divinely gifted and separate from society has been challenged), but clearly problematic when applied to a collaborative, mechanical form such as film.

These distinctions between the inimitable work produced by an individual and work which could be mass produced were part of the wider division between high art and popular culture. High art forms are characterized by an artist speaking to an elite audience in elite settings (art galleries, theatres, opera houses, etc.). Film was seen instead as a form of popular culture; it was mass produced for a mass audience and watched in crowded, dark cinemas. Art is supposed to be untainted by financial interests as the artist is driven to produce their masterpiece whether or not they are paid for it – hence the stereotype of the starving artist in a garret. In contrast, films are made for money, with film-makers often paid large amounts to produce them. In addition, because of the high cost of film-making, directors can only make films if they can get the financial backing; they aren't free to follow their artistic vision. One of the aims of auteur theory is to try to reconcile this seeming paradox, to show that an artist can exist in a commercial industry. In this context it made sense to look at the directors working in Hollywood, the largest film industry in the world and one explicitly run on the kind of production models found in any other factory. In the auteur theory, the Hollywood studio system provides a control for the great director as the auteur will be able to transcend the constraints of the system to express their personal vision.

The context of the high art versus popular culture debate suggests that it is more useful to see auteur theory as part of the argument for taking film seriously, for giving it the status of an art form, rather than as a literal description of the director as sole creator of the film. The definition of film as an art form was central to the founding ideas of auteur theory, which were expressed in a series of essays in the French film journal *Cahiers du Cinema* during the 1950s. In these essays, the critics developed an argument which became known as *la politique des* auteurs, which outlined what was wrong with French cinema and in doing so argued for the superiority of the Hollywood style. At this stage there was no 'theory' of authorship but rather a polemic; although important, the distinction between the two is often lost. A theory is a set of principles which explains a particular phenomenon or experience. Auteur theory is the attempt to explain how film works as an art form – it is the product of the director's vision – and to apply that across all films in all periods. It is, in other words, a total theory of film. A polemic, which is what the critics of *Cahiers du Cinema* were engaged in, is very different. It is a passionate and strongly worded argument about events in a particular place and time, in this case about the problems in the French film industry in the post-war period, not an attempt to explain everything about cinema. This polemic became translated into the 'auteur theory' by an American critic, Andrew Sarris, who used it in his survey of Hollywood cinema, *The American Cinema* (1968), to categorize hundreds of American directors into different levels of achievement.

The 'manifesto' for *la politique des auteurs* was François Truffaut's article 'A certain tendency of the French cinema' (1954), an attack on the post-war French film industry which he referred to disparagingly as the 'tradition of quality', or the '*cinema de papa*', and defined as contrived and wooden, projecting a bourgeois image of good taste and high culture. This was achieved through high production values, reliance on stars, genre conventions and the privileging of the script over the *mise en scène* (cited in Buckland, 2010, pp83–84). For Truffaut, the tradition of quality was a literary rather than a cinematic form; he described some of the leading film-makers of the day as 'essentially literary men and I reproach them here for being contemptuous of the cinema by underestimating it' (cited in Bordwell and Thomson, 1990). Jean-Luc Godard, addressing a meeting of directors at the Cannes Film Festival in 1957, told them: 'Your camera movements are ugly because your subjects are bad, your cast acts badly because your dialogue is worthless; in a word you don't know how to create cinema because you no longer even know what it is' (cited in Bordwell and Thomson, 1990). Instead, *la politique* called for a cinema which explored the language unique to cinema which would shake up the old ways of film-making, allowing a younger generation of directors to make films (of course, these new, young film-makers included Truffaut and Godard).

This attack on the French national cinema needs to be looked at in the context of the post-war French film industry. During the 1930s, French cinema had been at the pinnacle of international film culture with great film-makers such as Jean Renoir, Marcel Carné and Jean Cocteau. During the occupation of France during the war, the film industry was charged with producing Nazi propaganda and entertainment. Many of the directors and technicians of the time left France, taking their creativity and expertise; those who stayed were often unable to work after the war. Coinciding with this decline in national cinema, a flood of Hollywood films was released in France following the ban on US films during the war time occupation. In effect, French audiences were able to watch several years of Hollywood back catalogue, almost like an archive of Hollywood 'golden age' production. Seeing several John Ford or Alfred Hitchcock films in quick succession provided the context for an approach to film which relies on studying a director's body of work, not just individual films. The films admired by the *Cahiers* critics were in the main genre films – the kind of popular film-making usually ridiculed by the critics. But in the pages of *Cahiers de Cinema* these were treated as great films made by artists – or auteurs. To justify this belief the *Cahiers* critics attempted to shift Hollywood cinema from the status of popular commercial enterprise and to incorporate it within the realms of high art. They did this through assigning an author to the film, an individual whose vision of the world was apparent in their films. Not all directors are auteurs: it is an evaluative judgement. To be designated an auteur the director must show evidence of an individual vision across a substantial body of work, a worldview which could be detected in the consistent style and themes of their films. This was done through a detailed analysis of the *mise en scène*, where, it was argued, the personal style could be detected.

The development of the auteur theory has had a range of effects and influences. In terms of the growth of film studies as a discipline, it was fundamental in providing a framework for study. Courses could now be taught around the great directors and their films in a similar way to the study of literature; film had found its status as one of the arts. The dominance of the auteur theory also had more negative effects. It became a divisive theory of extremes with different groups arguing endlessly over which directors were and were not auteurs. The focus on the director of the film meant that other areas of film production – and reception – were ignored. This was particularly true in the context of audience studies. The auteur theory assumed that the meaning of a film is placed there by the director and that it is then transmitted to the audience *en masse*, an assumption which was challenged by the impact of genre theory in the 1980s. Outside of film studies, the influence of the auteur theory is clear (which makes it unusual for a theory) in the marketing of films and the emergence of the director as superstar. This is evident in the way that directors such as Steven Spielberg, Quentin Tarantino and Martin Scorsese are used to promote their films in much the same manner as stars were previously. It is also now common to use the idea of the auteur synonymously with director, so that even a first- or second-time director can be referred to in this way. Knowledge of the director of the film is also used by different parts of the audience to signal an expert knowledge about cinema; saying that you want to see the latest Alexander Payne film, rather than the latest George Clooney comedy, is stating your film studies expertise (or – some might say – being a film snob).

While we still routinely use the concept of auteur by referring to a film as belonging to its director (so deeply ingrained is this that even those who disagree with auteur theory are likely to do it), the validity of the theory itself is much less accepted now in academia. You are still likely to study it, but more in the context of its influential yet problematic nature. However, auteur theory is not completely extinct, but has been reinvigorated by opening up the definition of an auteur to include stars and institutions, and through the crossover with a new area of film studies – that of identity politics. In this new approach under the general title of authorship studies, the works of individual directors are analysed in the context of national, ethnic and gender identities, with previously marginalized film-makers such as Dorothy Arzner, Oscar Micheaux and John Waters being reappraised.

Challenges to the auteur theory

The dominance of the auteur theory was challenged by a group of British theorists during the late 1960s and 1970s. This group, university academics associated with the BFI, were influenced by recent developments in French theory, such as structuralism and psychoanalysis. They believed that this could be developed into a film theory which would provide much greater rigour to the study of film than the reliance on auteur theory.

The BFI is the central body in the transformation of the study of film from film analysis and authorship to film theory, and thus the expansion of film studies courses at universities. During this period the Education Department of the BFI was crucial in defining film studies as a discipline and promoting it in higher education. The aims of the department were to continue to provide support and guidance for existing film education programmes, which were mostly in schools, but to also give film studies an academic standing through writing about it in a theoretical way. This would increase the cultural value of film and would be achieved by the funding of film posts in universities and through the BFI publishing arm.

The film theory associated with BFI education developed through a combination of seminars, lectures and screenings; it was disseminated through BFI books and the journal *Screen*. Film theory was a move away from the previous approaches to teaching about film and was influenced by the developments in structuralism and narrative theories. Mulvey and Wollen (2008) argued that 'The theory of myth and narrativity . . . made it possible to think in an intellectual way about films made for mass distribution and entertainment', again pointing to the need to find a way to marry the traditionally disparate areas of high art and popular culture. In terms of theory this meant a shift from auteur theory to structuralism and semiotics with the application of the work of Strauss, Propp, Bazin and Metz, much of which – in various forms – has remained central to the practice of 'doing film'. The success of the project to reinforce the status of film studies as a theoretical discipline created tensions with those involved in film education in a broader context. The main areas of conflict were to do with what should be studied as the new theorists championed Hollywood cinema over European art film. More profound and lasting was the division between the way in which film studies was taught in universities compared with schools and film societies, for example, with a great divide opening up between proponents of theory and those who questioned its usefulness. For the latter, the gap between semiotic and structuralist analysis of Hollywood films and the actual audience experience of watching films was too great to be acceptable.

Summary

- There have been programmes of film study since the beginning of the twentieth century.
- The first film courses focused on technical skills and the idea of moral uplift.
- Film was not seen as worthy of study due to its status as popular culture rather than high art.
- The auteur theory provided the framework for an academic approach to film and therefore the first film studies courses at university.
- With the development of film theory in the 1960s and 1970s, a division emerged between the subject as taught at university and in schools, film societies, etc.

References and further reading

Bordwell, D. and Thompson, K. (1990) *Film Art: An Introduction*, McGraw-Hill, New York, NY

Buckland, W. (2010) *Understand Film Studies*, Hodder Education, London

Hodgkinson, A. et al (1950) *School Film Appreciation*, British Film Institute, London

Mulvey, L. and Wollen, P. (2008) 'From cinephilia to film studies', in L. Grieveson and H. Wassen (eds) *Inventing Film Studies*, Duke University Press, Durham, NC

Polan, D. (2007) *Scenes of Instruction: The Beginnings of the U.S. Study of Film*, University of California Press, Berkeley, CA

Sarris, A. (1968) *The American Cinema 1929–1968*, Da Capo Press, Cambridge, MA

Staiger, J. (1985) 'The politics of film canons', *Cinema Journal*, vol 24, no 3, pp4–23

The historiography of film studies is an increasingly important area of research. In addition to Polan's history of film courses in the US and Grieveson and Wassen's collection of essays referred to above, see also Terry Bolas's *Screen Education: From Film Education to Media Studies* (Intellect Books, 2009). Bolas traces the development of film studies in the UK, from the post-war period, through the setting up of the BFI, to its current status as a university subject among media and cultural studies. The book also includes a detailed timeline of key developments in screen education.

The British Film Institute has an extensive archive of reports, conference papers and early syllabi from the first film studies courses. Some of these are available online at http://www.bfi.org.uk/filmtvinfo/publications/education_publications.html. The full collection is at the BFI Library in London: http://www.bfi.org.uk/filmtvinfo/library.

3

The History of the Canon

The Development (and Deconstruction) of the Film Studies Canon

In this chapter we will consider:

- What is a canon and why is it necessary?
- What criteria are used in admitting films to the canon?
- Why are canons controversial?
- Do canons change over time?
- Are canons nationally specific?

Film studies as a subject has an unusual relationship to canon formation. This is due to the overlap in film studies of different constituencies – academics, critics, industry and audiences – all of which have influenced the construction of the canon and argued over what is worthy of study. This influence of non-academic practice on canon formation once again highlights the distinctive place that film studies has in academia. It is also true that it is the nature of cinema as an industry which fuelled the need to construct a canon in the first place, to prove that cinema was an art form which could be studied, and not just a business. Canons are increasingly controversial because they are seen as elitist categories which ignore large parts of a subject area, but they are still the foundation of any academic discipline.

In his essay on the state of the film canon at the end of the twentieth century, 'Canon fodder', Paul Schraeder (2006: 35), a director, scriptwriter and film historian, sums up the controversies and contradictions inherent in the historical role and contemporary place of canons:

The notion of a canon, any canon – literary, musical, painting – is 20th-century heresy. There is much debate about the canons but no agreement. Not only is there no agreement about what a canon should include, there's no agreement about whether there should be canons at all. Or, if there is agreement, it is this: canons are bad – elitist, sexist, racist, outmoded, and politically incorrect. Yet, *de facto* film canons exist – in abundance. They exist in college curriculums, they exist in yearly 10-best lists, they exist in best-of-all-time lists of every sort.

This is the paradox of the canon: it is theoretically discredited but also indispensable. Schraeder points to another irony peculiar to film studies: that it was the new technology of cinema which, in part, led to the call for the destruction of artistic canons in the first place. The advent of new technologies such as photography and film blurred the boundaries of traditional definitions of art on which canon formation had been based. 'Here then is the problem: how can you have a film canon when the very existence of motion pictures played a decisive role in the collapse of the canon?' (Schraeder, 2006: 41). This questioning of the process of canon formation while also recognizing the need for canons has become a popular way of incorporating the outmoded aspects of the canon within contemporary film studies.

A canon in any subject is an agreed list of works, ideas and theoretical approaches which are studied within that subject area. They are the elements which constitute a discipline. The word canon is a religious term meaning rule or law, and refers to the teachings of the scriptures. The Bible, therefore, is made up of the canonical works of Christianity. This use of a religious term for a secular academic study has often been remarked upon, and the formation of academic secular canons began in the eighteenth century, coinciding with the decline of religious art. The connotations of the religious meaning of the term, though, have remained. In defining what constitutes a canonical art work, the emphasis on its uniqueness and beauty often suggests a divine rather than man-made creation. In film studies this is evident in authorship theory, where the director is considered the creator of great works.

The canon in film studies refers to a group of films and directors deemed worthy of study, being the most valuable in the history of cinema. This group of films and film-makers will be the ones that, as a student, you will be expected to be familiar with and to have an opinion on, even by people who believe that the canon is an outdated concept. In addition, particular theories, such as authorship and genre, can also be identified as part of the canon, and these have a great influence on the films chosen. In Chapter 1 we identified some of the films which are regularly referred to as 'the best' or 'most important' by academics and critics. The majority of film studies degree courses cover a similar range of theoretical approaches and content, indicating the importance and influence of a canon. In his analysis of the history of the canon for the British Film Institute's magazine *Sight and Sound*, the film historian Ian Christie demonstrates why the canon is important:

> not only does the canon directly govern what future generations of students will learn about, but indirectly it affects what is bought for television, what's programmed in cinematheques and repertory cinemas, what's released on video, what appears in cinema related publishing and, perhaps most important, what archives prioritise and preserve. (Christie, 1992, p31)

The practical need for a canon is well established: without one, the study of film would be an impossible task as there would be no way of navigating the hundreds of thousands of films available. For some, canon formation is therefore simply an innocent and practical activity which provides a framework for study. However, this common-sense argument in favour of the canon soon becomes problematic as there isn't one canon which can be looked up, referred to and agreed upon. An alternative view to the 'common-sense' approach argues that canon construction isn't simply a pragmatic activity, but is a process whereby a culture singles out work which it believes to be of high quality and value. The argument that the canon is based on value judgement rather than a simple system of categorization is now well established. The controversial nature of the canon derives from the debate over how it is formed. Do the films included represent a universal measurement of worth, their quality evident to everyone? Or does the choice reflect the view of a particular group whose values are shaped by a particular social and cultural context? Christie (1992, p31) argues that the contemporary canon has its roots in the 1960s and 1970s: 'the current version seems to me to be very much a product of the 60s and 70s that itself gave birth to modern academic film studies'. This argument – that canons are a product of a time and place rather than a representation of universal values – has particular importance because once a canon has been formed it becomes reinforced and repeated, making it difficult to challenge or change.

The canon in practice

Chapter 1 gave a range of examples of where the canon can be located, including university course content, as well as critics' and audience's 'best of' lists, such as the *Sight and Sound* series. The criteria for judging which films (and/or film-makers) are to be included or omitted in these contexts is rarely made explicit. In compiling their book *Key Film Texts*, film lecturers Graham Roberts and Heather Wallis (2002) attempt to clarify the process which led to their choice of 50 films which they felt film students should study. The authors' stated aim is for the chosen films to provide a curriculum of study which would give students a sense of the history of the subject in order to be able to analyse film in a meaningful way.

Their criteria begins with selection based on the understanding that the canon provides a 'grounding, a common pool of references in which we can base our investigations into cinema' (Roberts and Wallis, 2002, p2); therefore, their selection must include films already recognized as great. This demonstrates the danger that the canon can be restrictive and stagnate; films have to be studied because they have always been studied, which allows little opportunity for new films to enter the canon, college curriculum, etc. In Roberts and Wallis's list, this 'reproducing canon' is evident in the inclusion of *Intolerance*, whose director D. W. Griffith has been part of the canon since its earliest formation. Other films recognizable from the history of the canon include *Battleship Potemkin*, *The Gold Rush*, *Citizen Kane* and *Bicycle Thieves*. It also draws on the familiar parameters of canonization in its emphasis on Hollywood and European cinema, with only two films from outside of these areas: *The Seven Samurai* (Japan, 1954) and *Chungking Express* (Hong Kong, 1997). The list also bases selection on the inclusion of films by recognized auteurs, with three (*Rear Window*, *Vertigo* and *Psycho*) by Alfred Hitchcock, making him the most represented (and therefore best?) director. In other ways the list subverts traditional definitions of a canon. The shared characteristics of canonical films identified in Chapter 1 are a product of aesthetic and ideological analysis. The best films were deemed as such because they were formally experimental, visually stunning and technically breath-taking, or carried important messages about society. Films such as *Star Wars*, *Jurassic Park* and *Raiders of the Lost Ark*, which also feature on the *Key Film Texts* list, may not meet these criteria (although that immediately reminds us of the subjectivity of these judgements), but are included for what they say about the changing nature of film style, the film industry and its audience. In this the list mirrors developments in the teaching and study of film, where film production and reception are now seen as important areas of study. The influence of theories of postmodernism is evident in the widening scope of this list, with films selected for their representation of groups outside of the hegemonic culture. This includes feminist and queer cinema

(*The Piano*, *All about My Mother*), African-American film-making (*Do the Right Thing*) and the recognition of popular genre films (*The Matrix*, *The Blair Witch Project*). In this way, the *Key Film Texts* list is typical of the contemporary approach to canon construction, drawing on traditional entries while trying to open up the range of films which are considered eligible for study, particularly with reference to groups who have not been represented previously.

History of canon formation

Through an examination of the shared characteristics of canonical films and the wider context of canon formation across disciplines, film theorists have identified a range of possible criteria which are used in canon formation. The earliest entries into the film studies canon during the 1920s were, it is now argued, inherently conservative because the selections did not take into account the distinctive nature of film as a form. Instead, traditional definitions of art were used to 'prove' that film was an art form, and therefore comparable to the other fine arts. These traditional definitions rested on the concepts of harmony and beauty, the effect of which was to provide moral uplift, ideas that probably now seem very old fashioned and have little connection to film. This attempt to force film to fit existing definitions of art, rather than to redefine them, provided the context for the dominant theoretical approach to film: that of authorship, which saw the director as an artist who transmitted their view of the world through film (see Chapter 2 for more on the history and influence of authorship theory). The conception of film as art had consequences for the canon because films were included based on aesthetics and moral purpose, characteristics which were claimed as universal but were, in fact, the product of an elite group. In her influential essay outlining the limitations of the film studies canon, 'The politics of film canons', the film historian Janet Staiger (1985) argues that the first attempts to construct a canon were, in part, the result of financial motivation. The existence of a canon conferred respectability and jobs on the early film critics and theorists, as well as making film a reputable art for a middle-class audience to consume.

Politics of selection

Any form of canon formation involves a process of selection and omission which has an influence over how the subject is taught and understood. Staiger

(1985) identifies three rationales for canon formation: efficiency, creating order from chaos and evaluation. Each of these rationales has a range of consequences.

The efficiency criterion aids the study of film as it institutionalizes a group of films which academics and writers can assume the reader has knowledge of; this list then becomes part of a shared understanding of the makeup of the subject. However, the consequence of this function of the canon is that it can lead, in Staiger's words, to 'sloppy thinking'. When a film (or film-maker) is canonized, people soon accept rather than question their status – it becomes fact. Staiger uses the example of the status of D. W. Griffith to illustrate this effect. Griffith was one of the first canonical film-makers. His body of work (*Birth of a Nation*, *Intolerance*, etc) was valued for its aesthetic form and technical mastery rather than the subject and themes of his work. This approach is evident in Andrew Sarris's (1968) study of US auteurs, *The American Cinema*, where Griffiths is included in the highest category, one of the 'Pantheon' directors. In his evaluation of Griffith as a director, Sarris emphasizes the way in which the director uses the form of film language (editing, framing, lighting, etc.) to create meaning and compares this to an established art form – that of poetry:

> Griffith devised a grammar of emotions through his expressive editing. The focal length of his lens became a function of feeling. Close ups not only intensified an emotion; they shifted characters from the republic of prose to the kingdom of poetry. Griffith's privileged moments are still among the most beautiful in all cinema. They belong to him alone, since they are beyond mere technique. Griffith invented this 'mere' technique, but he also transcended it. (Sarris, 1968, p52)

The widespread acceptance of this analysis of Griffith as a pioneer, a unique individual, is still evident decades after Sarris wrote his analysis and is accepted by other disciplines, such as history. In the *Organization of American Historians Magazine of History*, Paul Dennis Hoffman (1986) discusses the use of *Birth of a Nation* as a teaching tool and contextualizes it by stating that, in the film, 'Griffith utilised for the first time in one motion picture techniques such as close up, long shot, the fade out, flash back, night photography and back lighting.'

Due to the emphasis on form over content in the film studies canon, *Birth of a Nation*, with its celebration of the Ku Klux Klan's role in defending the Southern states in the American Civil War, became part of the canon. The basis for canonization rested in large part on Griffith's claim to a unique status as the first film-maker to use a variety of technical innovations, making him a pioneer whom others then followed. So ingrained did this idea become that even when the inclusion of *Birth of a Nation* in the canon was criticized, it was still done in the context of the film being a unique work. Donald Bogle, in his analysis of the construction of black stereotypes in Hollywood entitled 'Beginnings: From *Uncle Tom's Cabin* to the *Birth of a Nation*' (2001), is highly critical of the racist ideology of the film and its use of damaging stereotypes which have remained influential: 'Griffith propagated the myth of slave contentment and made it appear as if slavery had elevated the negro from his bestial instincts' (Bogle, 2001, p10). But Bogle also continues the canonical definition of Griffith as a remarkable film-maker: 'It altered the entire course and concept of American movie making, developing the close up, cross cutting, rapid fire editing, the iris, the split-screen shot and realistic and impressionistic editing' (Bogle, 2001, p10).

Evidence which contradicted this account of Griffith as the 'first' was found in the work of film-makers outside of the canon who had used the same techniques at the same time or even before Griffiths; but this got little recognition due to the dominance of the canon. As Staiger (1985, p9) argues: 'Griffith's feature films and contemporary publicity (for which he was in part responsible) led some writers to the conclusion that he was first to achieve a number of technical innovations and, following that, that he was the only one and thus influenced the rest of the industry.' The demands of efficiency meant that, in practice, a mistake, a piece of 'sloppy thinking', became institutionalized. Staiger argues that canonization is so strong, the idea that a film-maker might be replaced so unimaginable, that the terms of Griffith's inclusion were refined rather than his inclusion questioned. Therefore, the argument for Griffith's place in the canon became based on the argument that while he may not have been the only person to use these innovations, he was the first to really understand their function, returning him to his unique position and therefore to the canon. In this process, canon formation leads to an implicit (at times explicit) denigration of other films and film-makers. For Griffith to be great, other film-makers had to be inferior. Through this example it is clear that even the pragmatic justification for canon formation – that it is efficient – has a range of negative effects.

The second rationale for canon formation, the creation of order from chaos, is a related and apparently practical approach. As with the efficiency rationale, it is vital in creating a manageable area of study:

33

Grouping, classifying, and finding typicality are long-honored and traditional pursuits in the acquisition of knowledge. Hence, large numbers of films are more easily handled if certain generalizing characteristics are determined. The idea of 'Renaissance painting' or 'realist drama' or 'American horror films' provides a grip on a large and historically specific group of objects. (Staiger, 1985, p10)

In canon formation the chosen films become exemplars rather than typical examples; they are held up as the best of their period, style, genre, etc. rather than remaining an objective classification of types. This again has the effect of denigrating, by omission, all the other entries in the same classification. This could perhaps be avoided if the examples chosen were selected at random. For example, from a list of every western ever made, we could choose every third one to represent the genre in the canon. But even this is rife with problems. Is it so easy to define which films are westerns and which are not? Is the western a Hollywood or international form? Should there be westerns from Japan and Italy, as well as from American cinema? Do all countries define the western in the same way? It is also the case that the initial selection of which categories to include, whether by genre, style, period, studio, etc., is based on a value judgement. In the early days of film studies, genre films were seen as less important than art cinema, and even when genre began to be taken seriously as an area of study, it was the gangster and the western which were studied. The melodrama and the woman's film, for example, were only admitted into the canon due to feminist analysis and argument. The very process of picking categories is in itself evaluative, which, Staiger contends, is the third and overarching criterion for selection.

As is evident in the example of selection by classification, evaluation in constructing a canon is unavoidable. Staiger's answer to this conundrum is to foreground how the evaluative criteria work and to ask a series of questions about canons. Doing this is part of an ideological approach to canons which makes visible the processes involved in canon formation. This method is in opposition to the auteur approach, which has been the dominant theory in canon formation. In the discussion in Chapter 1 of authorship, it became clear that an auteur critic values the characteristics of uniqueness, universality and transcendence in film. Directors – and their films – are valued because they move beyond the specific context of their place and time of production to create works which are everlasting. These films are the product of an elite group – Sarris's 'Pantheon' of directors. These works are great because they embody enduring values which have a positive social effect on the audience;

it is the idea that great art works (such as great films) exert a positive moral effect. One of the criticisms of the auteur theory is that auteur critics see their subjective judgements as being 'true', as representing the positions with which everyone must agree. In this way, the canonization of particular directors appears natural, as if it is self-evident that these are the greatest directors producing the greatest films. This naturalization has the effect of reinforcing the values of a hegemonic culture – white, male, middle class, western – and ignoring the voices of groups outside of it. This was particularly damaging because the certainty of the auteur canon in effect closed down further discussion and research. To counter this Staiger (1985) suggests a group of questions which should be asked by anyone studying films from the canon or involved in canon formation:

- What standards are used to make moral judgements?
- Who determines the social good?
- Are the standards for everyone (are there any groups who are not represented)?
- What about those outside of the hegemonic culture (represented by the auteur critics)?

Canons and national cinemas

In addition to the efficiency, organizational and evaluative rationales which are part of the process of canon formation, canons are also a product of specific nations and cultures, and serve different functions in different cultures. The canon referred to in this and previous chapters is really an Anglo-American canon rather than a French or Spanish one, and canon formation is itself a western practice. The national and cultural specificity of canons has a variety of effects, not just on the makeup of the canon itself, but also on national cinemas. Ian Christie (1992) argues that when British and French canons include American films, thereby valuing them more highly than their national cinemas, it can have detrimental effects. By critically acclaiming Hollywood films, which are already dominant in British and French cinemas, it may encourage a negative view of national product, seeing it as inferior to Hollywood cinema. A related effect is the treating of national cinema as a 'protected' form which should be judged by different (less rigorous?) criteria than other entries in the canon.

The marginalized position of British cinema in the canon is evident in the *Sight and Sound* poll of 'Greatest Films', which is released every decade.

These lists have never included a British film in the top ten; the highest placed British film in the 2012 list is *The Third Man* (Carol Reed, 1949) at number 73. In the *Cahiers du Cinema* list of the 100 greatest films of all time there are no British films, but the top 20 includes 10 Hollywood and 4 French films. The domination of the French canon by Hollywood cinema may seem surprising given the national pride felt in France for its films and film industry. It is more understandable, though, in the context of the post-war film industry. During this period, influential critics writing in *Cahiers du Cinema* (some of whom, such as Truffaut and Godard, went on to be film directors) attacked the French cinema of the time for being dull and worthy, particularly in comparison with the Hollywood genre films of auteurs such as Hawks, Ford and Hitchcock. Most of the Hollywood films in the *Cahiers du Cinema* list are from the immediate post-war decades and by those directors.

The film studies canon has therefore been dominated by Hollywood and European cinema; but Europe has only been partially represented, with the emphasis on France and Italy, and such canonical movements as Italian neo-realism and the French new wave. One of the aims of questioning the process of canon formation has been to admit a wider group of European and non-European national cinemas. This has often been influenced by the politics of those involved in canon formation. During the 1970s, film theory in the UK was influenced by Marxism and post-structuralism, which resulted in an interest in radical film-making, distrust in the elitism of canon formation and a desire to overturn the existing canonical works. This led to what has been termed the 'counter-canon', which included films which had previously been ignored by canons and film history, in general. These included films by women film-makers, neglected genres and 'Third Cinema', particularly the revolutionary films of Latin America.

The concept of the counter-canon recognized the limitations of the traditional canon, but also realized the impossibility of eradicating it completely. The interest in films outside of Hollywood and European cinemas has continued – although these 'new' cinemas have never challenged the original's dominance – with a range of national cinemas (including Chinese, Hong Kong, African and Iranian) becoming part of the canon over the last 30 years. The inclusion of 'non-western' cinemas has been as controversial as its previous non-inclusion. Accusations of a colonialist approach have been levelled at the idea of 'discovering' an existing cinema and legitimizing it through inclusion in the western canon. The recognition of different types of national cinemas also continues the debate around the evaluative and elitist nature of the canon; the films chosen to represent these national cinemas are rarely the ones watched by a mass audience in those countries.

The canon today: Different types of canon

In *Light My Fire: The Geology and Geography of Film Canons*, the film critic Adrian Martin (2001) surveys the state of canons today, arguing that there are two canons now in general use: 'the *Star Wars* canon' and 'the [*Citizen*] *Kane* canon'. He then proposes that there should be a third canon, 'the Kiarostami canon' (named after the avant-garde Iranian director), which would include all the areas ignored by the other two, particularly experimental non-western films. Martin's argument is fuelled by an attack on the commercial nature of the *Star Wars* canon and frustration at the stagnation of the *Kane* canon. The former is shaped by film industry interests – although it claims to be based on popular taste – with Hollywood blockbusters dominating. This commercialization of the canon, which has a business rather than educational rationale, is a concern for many critics and theorists. The sometimes controversial film critic Jonathan Rosenbaum, who is a proponent of canon formation, argues that a canon based on box office success will have a detrimental effect on the wider film culture, both among audiences and academics. In 'List-o-Mania, Or how I Stopped Worrying and Learned to Love American Movies' (Rosenbaum, 1998) he addresses the role of the American Film Institute's 100 best films in film culture, a list which included only American films that had been box office successes: 'What does matter is the rise of corporate cultural initiatives bent on selling and reselling what we already know and have, making every alternative appear more scarce and esoteric, and not even attempting to expand or illuminate the choices made in the process.' In contrast, the *Kane* canon is full of 'great films' (*Sight and Sound* and *Cahiers du Cinema* 'best film' lists are examples of the *Kane* canon). But, Martin (2001) points out, canonization 'tends to mummify or ossify film classics. It is too reverential. Everyone knows that when young students sit down to watch a film thinking, "oh, this is some old classic that I am supposed to appreciate as a great work of art", they are already dead to what that film can offer them.'

In proposing a new canon it is important to consider what it is that a canon should do, whether it is pedagogical in providing the foundation for film study, or commercial, helping to sell cinema tickets, DVDs, online streaming, etc. For Rosenbaum and Martin, the canon is pedagogical and essential, as Martin (2001) states:

I do think that canons worth anything, new or old, are pedagogical – which is nothing to be ashamed of. In a canon, critics and programmers and Film Festival or Cinémathèque directors take on the authority of being public teachers, they stand up and shout: this is what you, the audience, must see, what you must know, what you must experience. The commercial *Star Wars* canon, on the contrary, isn't about pedagogy, it's only about confirming what the mass of people already see and know and do.

The canon, despite being an apparently outdated concept, is still the foundation of film studies courses and wider film education. It is fought over and expanded, but the central idea remains: that there are a group of films and film-makers which are the best and which you as a film studies student should be aware of.

Summary

- The canon plays an evaluative as well as a practical classifying role in film studies.
- The canon values particular types of films – Hollywood and European, those directed by men, feature length, dramas – over others.
- Canons have different functions in different nations.
- The traditional film canon is not a universal reflection of great films but the product of the values of a particular group in a particular time and place.
- The canon has been opened up to include a wider variety of film styles, national cinemas and representations, but not destroyed.

References and further reading

Bogle, D. (2001) 'Beginnings: From *Uncle Tom's Cabin* to the *Birth of a Nation*', in D. Bogle *Toms, Coons, Mulattoes, Mammies and Bucks: An Interpretive History of Blacks in American Films*, fourth edition, Continuum International Publishing Group, London and New York

Christie, I. (1992) 'Canon fodder', *Sight and Sound*, December, pp31–33

Hoffman, P. D. (1986) 'The birth of a nation and the civil rights movement of the 1950s and 1960s: A teaching strategy', *Organization of American Historians Magazine of History*, vol 2, no 1, summer, pp37–39

Martin, A. (2001) *Light My Fire: The Geology and Geography of Film Canons*, June, Senses of Cinema, http://www.sensesofcinema.com/contents/01/14/light_my_fire.html, accessed 14 February 2012

Roberts, G. and Wallis, H. W. (2002) *Key Film Texts*, Arnold, New York, NY

Rosenbaum, J. (1998) 'List-o-Mania, Or how I Stopped Worrying and Learned to Love American Movies', 25 June, *Chicago Reader*, http://www.chicagoreader.com/chicago/list-o-mania/Content?oid=896619, accessed 23 April 2012

Sarris, A. (1968) *The American Cinema: Directors and Directions, 1929–1968*, De Capo Press, New York, NY

Schraeder, P. (2006) 'Canon fodder', *Film Comment*, September–October, pp33–48

Staiger, J. (1985) 'The politics of film canons', *Cinema Journal*, vol 24, no 3, pp4–23

In *Essential Cinema: On the Necessity of Film Canons* (Johns Hopkins Press, 2004), Jonathan Rosenbaum argues for the importance of canons and puts forward a range of films from different periods and places as worthy of inclusion. For Rosenbaum, the canon is an important way of challenging the homogeneous Hollywood style, which is driven by commercialization.

Alexander Doty, one of the founders and most influential writers on queer theory, analyses canonical films from a queer perspective, a process he refers to as *Flaming Classics* (Routledge, 2000).

The most recent *Sight and Sound* 'Best Film' poll is published in the September 2012 issue. In the run-up to the announcement of the results, the magazine published a series of essays by academics and critics on contenders for the list. Examples include:

- Hannah McGill (May 2012) 'Blood and sand: *Beau travail*', http://www.bfi.org.uk/sightandsound/feature/49855;
- B. Kite (March 2012) 'Remain in light: Mulholland Dr. and the cosmogony of David Lynch', http://www.bfi.org.uk/sightandsound/feature/49820.

4

Key Approaches

Genre Theory

In this chapter we will consider:

- What is the relationship between auteur and genre theory?
- Which genres have been the focus of academic study?
- Why have some genres been ignored?
- What is the role of the audience in genre theory?
- How do we know which film belongs to which genre?

Having looked at the importance of auteur theory in forming the film canon, it would be useful to consider where academics went next in mapping out the terrain for the study of film. Much like auteur theory, genre theory was born out of a desire to label, group and classify, seeking to organize the world of cinema into neat compartments as a basis for close study. Genre theory set out to address certain shortcomings of auteur theory by embracing popular cinema rather than seeking works of art in the work of auteurs.

The study of film genre became a central theoretical concern from the late 1960s and into the following decade, influenced by the work of André Bazin and Tom Ryall, among others. Genre study can provide fundamental insights into the film industry and audiences in comparison to auteur theory, offering the opportunity to deal with cinema as both an industrial and a popular medium. There was a perceived elitism implicit in the auteur approach, as the only films deemed worthy of study were those which could be argued to be part of a body of work produced by the artist/director, displaying their signature of creativity and artistry. Whereas auteur theory approached the film as a work of art, exploring the imprint of the director as artist, it overlooked the industrial and audience context of the film, an imbalance which genre theory attempted to redress.

All too often the genre road could lead back to the auteur, with films being considered in the light of how the 'auteur' had established their signature within a specific genre. One might consider *The Searchers* in terms of its genre identity as a western, yet go on to analyze its status as a John Ford western, to be evaluated alongside Ford's prolific output in the genre, such as *Stagecoach*, *My Darling Clementine* and *Red River*. Genre theory offers a different approach to auteur theory; in practice, the two can be seen to intersect each other, both seeking to explore, analyse and shed light on the film text, yet revealing different dimensions, enhancing our ultimate understanding.

What is genre theory?

> Genre: Kind, type; esp. a style or category of painting, novel, film, etc., characterized by a particular form or purpose.
>
> (*Oxford English Dictionary*)

We all have an understanding of different types of films, using familiar labels to describe a particular film: horror, chick flick, thriller, etc. The labelling of films is important in marketing a film to its audience, drawing on our recognition of these different types and forming expectations which we hope will be gratified by the viewing experience. In this respect, genre is about branding and packaging a product; it is part of the business of film. Yet genre has also been part of the academic study of texts since the beginnings of literary criticism. For example, the idea of genre in literature can be dated back to Ancient Greece, and the division of literary writings into three major types – lyric, drama and epic – according to the subject matter and treatment thereof (that is, the internal and external dynamics of the text).

Whereas auteur theory sought to construct a critical claim that film can be art, genre theory attempts to gain credence for the study of film in developing a scientific approach. The word 'genre' is derived from the Latin 'genus', a term used in biology as 'a basic taxonomic grouping . . . which contains a number of related and morphologically similar species . . . Formerly used in the classification of mineral, chemical substances, etc.', according to the

Oxford English Dictionary (2007). Such an approach suggests a rigid, systematic discipline in categorizing different 'species' of film, which does not seem to fit with the fluid and evolving nature of cinema. Some genres are easier to label than others in having a very distinct form, such as the western or the gangster film. Should there be set criteria by which each manifestation of a genre has to abide? What about the films that elude easy generic labelling? Can there be a fixed and defined list of genres which should be adhered to in classifying film?

The genre cycle

The work to define and make solid a body of knowledge surrounding genre has repeatedly encountered resistance, whether it be in placing a film within a specific genre or developing the fundamental taxonomy for genre analysis. One area of debate surrounded the idea of the 'genre cycle', suggesting that genres have a life cycle in that they attain maturity as they gain popularity, reaching an apotheosis in terms of realization of the genre form before becoming 'bastardized', decaying into parody and effectively dying out altogether. The concept uses the language of biology, seeking to contain and define genre with all the certainty and logic of a scientific principle. But the perennial problem with genre, in practice, is that it is too broad and undisciplined to 'fit', as we will see.

Genres were believed to evolve, not staying static but developing and changing over time. André Bazin, one of the earliest influential film genre theorists, developed his arguments with reference to the western, as indicated in his 1971 essay *The Evolution of the Western*. Bazin held that the western had reached a period of perfection in the 1930s and 1940s, in classics such as *Stagecoach* (1940), before the genre became less 'pure' as it sought to maintain appeal and interest, increasingly departing from typical themes and conventions. *High Noon* (1952) exemplified this, having received much criticism from genre purists for not including enough of the action, violence and settings associated with the western, and featuring extensive existential dialogue, postponing all action until the end.

The western proves to be a telling case study, undergoing a dramatic decline in the 1980s after having been one of the most popular Hollywood genres since the silent era. The western has survived, but not as a popular genre form, being more likely to be made for the art house audience, as with the crop of contemporary examples such as *The Assassination of Jesse James* (2007), *Meek's Cutoff* (2011) and *True Grit* (2011). The genre continues to make an appearance in Hollywood mainstream within a hybridized form – for example, as the context for the Will Smith action comedy *The Wild Wild West* (1999). The hybrid genre is not necessarily a new phenomenon in the cinema, as can be seen by earlier variations on the western form, such as *Blazin' Saddles* (1974), a comedy western, and *Seven Brides for Seven Brothers* (1954), a musical western.

In an oblique way the concept of genre evolution touches on the production practices of Hollywood, where production is cyclical, always seeking to build on trends in terms of box office success. The financially successful film may well result in other films attempting to replicate the formula for success, ultimately declining as the initial formula wanes in popularity. Yet the academic approach to the concept of genre evolution often failed to take into account the financial and industrial environment, being more concerned with studying the internal dynamics of the genre rather than its broader context.

Defining the genre

Central to the debates around genre was the dilemma as to how to define a genre – what tools and criteria could be used to pin down a rather elusive concept. Iconography was central to this activity in the exploration of how the 'outer form' of a genre consisted of specific visual elements which could be utilized by the director in order to create genre familiarity, along with the innovation needed to appeal to audiences. For many of the genre theorists, the western had provided a straightforward template with which to hone their critical tools, lending itself to the task with its strong visual imagery: vast empty desert plains, saloon bars filled with goodtime gals and an extensive bar to slide the customer's whiskey along, horses, guns, sheriff badges, the dusty main street of a deserted settlement, a few wagons and a mass of whooping Native Americans carrying bows and arrows.

Unfortunately, not all genres were quite so obliging in having such distinct iconography as the western and the gangster film – the genres which proved central to the genre theory of the 1960s and 1970s. It can be rather more challenging, for example, to come up with a definitive iconography for the comedy or action genres. Some genres were overlooked and dismissed, effectively constructing a rather exclusive critical landscape for popular cinema, where certain genres dominated critical thinking and were thus given validity. This exclusivity reveals certain flaws in the theory, with some generic labels, such as comedy, proving too broad to be useful. On the other hand, some genres proved too narrow to be useful, such as the grouping of biopics of Queen Victoria.

In addition to this, there appears to be a gender imbalance at play in these early genre studies, perhaps reflecting the inherently patriarchal nature of film academia and the lowly status of 'women's films'. One example of this was the failure to engage with the romance genre, even though it continues to be a vital constituent of Hollywood's output. Christine Gledhill's work on melodrama helped to lead the way in tackling the poor critical standing of this genre, leading to the critical re-evaluation of 'women's film'. Much of the early work on genre focused on Hollywood and shied away from the problematic nature of national cinemas. Theorists largely ignored the manifestation of genre forms outside Hollywood as well as failing to consider how audiences in other countries and cultures positioned themselves regarding Hollywood genres.

Genre and canon

The key problem which perennially derails genre theory is the difficulty in fixing the definition and nature of a genre. Iconography is one way in approaching genre, but does not work for all genres. Is there a pre-established iconography for each genre, or is there a film which can be held to exemplify the genre and can act as a template against which to compare others? Who establishes the nature of a genre? For what purpose?

Bazin led the way in genre theory by pinpointing a small number of films – including *Stagecoach*, *Virginia City* (1940) and *Western Union* (1941) – which he felt embodied the essence of the western. He effectively proposed a western canon, against which all other examples of the genre could be compared, arguing that the films manifested a purity of generic form which serves as a prototype. This was central to Bazin's work in studying the historical development of the western and its patterns, structures and key themes. Yet, this method of approach suggested a hierarchy in terms of purity of genre form, serving to evaluate films in comparison with the 'classics' and thus being effectively an exclusive approach to the study of film. This approach was very influential in genre studies as theorists sought to define a particular genre by identifying a canon of films which demonstrated its purest form.

Whose genre?

The problem with genre theory which Bazin's approach served to exemplify was the issue as to who actually decides genre categories: the theorist, audience or industry? And how useful is such an approach anyway? Much of the early work of genre criticism seemed to reflect the theorists' interests and agenda in mapping out the cinema of relevance to them, rather than actually engaging with the film industry and audiences, and in how genre theory could help to understand popular film in practice.

There has been a tendency for the theory to impose its own genre map onto popular film, starting from an academic framework, rather than the practices of the film industry. The film industry is pragmatic in terms of utilizing genre conventions in a flexible way in order to respond to audience tastes. Genre categorization is always in flux, being revised to capitalize on box office trends. The fluid nature of genre in practice is at odds with the early theorists' identification of films which could be considered 'classic' forms of their genre. The conservative nature of early genre criticism cannot accommodate the complex and 'layered' nature of popular film forms.

Genre classification can be a historical practice, with critics labelling film types and movements in retrospect, carrying out a process of genre revisionism. One example is the identification of the film noir by French critics, a label which was not widely used until the 1970s, and was clearly not in the minds of the Hollywood producers of the 1940s and 1950s. Indeed, films such as *Laura* (1944) and *Mildred Pierce* (1945) were thought of as melodramas at the time, while other examples of the genre were originally produced as crime thrillers, social problem or gangster films among other genres. The contention over film noir reveals many of the issues arising from genre criticism. Critics struggled to define the iconography of the genre, finding that the body of films encompassed an enormous diversity of settings, set pieces, situations and character types. The major determinant for a film to be deemed film noir is its visual style – low-key lighting, expressive *mise en scène*, monochrome cinematography and disorienting camera shots – although this has also been the cause of some controversy, as critics continue to debate whether specific films meet the criteria. Some critics have underscored the tensions around film noir by declaring that it is not a genre, but a 'style', while C. Jerry Kutner declares that 'When we talk about noir . . . we are talking about a vision, a way of seeing the world, that is transgeneric', suggesting that noir is a mode, similar to surrealism or expressionism, not a genre (Kutner, 2006).

The relationship between academic study and industrial practice is more complex than might initially appear to be the case. Genre studies had seemed to be a self-contained academic exercise which initially paid little attention to the industrial and popular experience of film. Yet the retrospective formation of a film noir canon suggested a more symbiotic relationship between the critic and the producer; films would consciously reference the tropes of the genre and would be marketed as 'noir'. The study of the genre provided a stylistic template for future film product by trading on film nostalgia and critical kudos, as with the marketing of the 'neo-noir' *LA Confidential* (1997) and the more offbeat independent film *Brick* (2005).

Genre and audience

The film industry is organized around an understanding of what types of films appeal to the audience. As a business, it needs to package its product to sell to the customer, who also has a clear sense of their preferences when deciding what to watch. This dynamic interplay between film, industry and audience is fundamental to cinema, long predating the work of genre theorists. A pragmatic understanding of genre has informed the film industry as it endeavours to engage an audience by building on the success of some films, and targeting specific audiences. In this respect, genre in practice is a means for the film industry to minimize risk by responding to public demand. A careful line has to be taken in ensuring that a film has a clear genre identity to brand it for its target audience, yet provides something different which will distinguish it enough from other films so as not to seem merely a rehash of a tired formula. The reliance on remakes and sequels is merely an extension, if not an intensification, of this process. The industry becomes so risk averse that it commissions films which have already been successful, merely extending the longevity of this success. The top ten box office films of 2010 reflects this: four of the films are sequels (*Toy Story 3*, *Iron Man 2*, *Twilight: Eclipse* and *Shrek Forever After*) and one film was a remake (*Karate Kid*).

In practice, genre forms are not mutually exclusive, tending to 'bleed' into each other as they share many elements. Genre is a fluid concept as producers seek to maximize the appeal of films to as wide an audience as possible. The blockbuster *Avatar* (2009) presents itself as a science fiction film with a narrative set in the future, featuring other worlds and futuristic technology. Yet, the film is classified as 'action/adventure/fantasy' on imdb.com, and features romance and war. The multi-generic nature of the film is not unusual and could perhaps be cited as contributing to the film's success. Steven Neale observed that 'nearly all Hollywood's films were hybrids insofar as they tended to combine one type of generic plot, a romance plot, with others' (Neale, 1990, p57). It is certainly the case that producers attempt to innovate and revive genres by developing new generic cocktails in the form of the hybrid genre. The western's popularity as a genre form peaked in the mid-twentieth century; but this does not prevent studios from endeavouring to revive it in new forms, such as the genre-busting *Cowboys and Aliens* (2011), which uses the Wild West as the setting for a science fiction film.

Beyond iconography

As we have seen, iconography was central to the process of genre definition, yet could become problematic with certain genres. Specific genres would share common elements that may go beyond the *mise en scène*, perhaps being defined by a performance style, subject matter, effect on the audience or even its stars. The genre of the musical is defined by a very specific style of performance, involving departures from verisimilitude as the narrative is suspended to allow sequences of singing and dancing. The melodrama and the comedy adapt narrative, performance and even style to engender a specific emotional response from the audience. Genres can even be defined by the particular audience whom they appear to target – for example, the melodrama is regarded as a 'women's film', in addition to being a 'weepie'. Certain stars become synonymous with specific genres and help to market the film to the target audience, becoming defined by the genre. Their star persona is moulded around the genre values and narratives, bringing a host of associations and consequent expectations built on their other performances. Thus, John Wayne and Henry Fonda came to define the western; Charlie Chaplin and Buster Keaton, the slapstick comedy; and Jennifer Aniston and Renée Zellweger, the contemporary romantic comedy.

Genre theory continued to develop to encompass influences from other areas, in particular the structuralist theories which had a profound impact upon film studies in the 1970s. Structuralism was primarily associated with linguistics but influenced academic thinking across a range of academic areas, including film. A structuralist approach sets out to analyse how meaning is conveyed by the structures and interrelationships of elements within the film. There was a growing interest in how repeated structural devices used across a genre could be analysed in terms of their sociocultural significance. For example, common narrative structures have been identified in the western which have been cited as evidence that the historical development of the genre relates to broader changes in American society.

Genre analysis started to develop a broader perspective, looking at common structures and formal characteristics across Hollywood cinema. Steve Neale's *Genre* (1980) hinged on the fundamental idea that all genres are variations of the conventions of classical narrative cinema, sharing common elements such as linear narrative development and closure, alongside recurrent discourses concerning romance, social order and the community. This approach to genre acknowledges the fundamental *similarities* that lie at the heart of Hollywood cinema, seeing genre distinctions as a different emphasis and approach in the deployment of traditional narrative devices. Most Hollywood films feature romance, for example; but different genres would give a different weighting and treatment to this narrative strand: a melodrama would foreground the romance, whereas an action/adventure film might use it as a subplot which complicates the central quest that the hero needs to complete.

The structuralist approach concluded that genre is very much a fluid concept, with common elements being shared across genres. The starting point for the study of a particular genre would be to discover what it has in common with other forms of Hollywood cinema rather than the differences which had been central to early genre criticism, which sought to capture the essence and exclusivity of a genre. It is no longer necessary to 'fix' a film within a particular genre category, but to analyse how the film's form utilizes the elements of classical narrative cinema in a way that may broadly fit within a genre, yet may stray into other genre territories. This approach to genre removes the problems inherent in trying to make films fit within a proscribed narrow range of genre categories. Genre analysis was moving towards recognizing how the film industry works, away from imposing an inflexible academic framework.

This can be seen from looking closely at the 2007 Disney film *Enchanted*, which superficially would seem to fit well within the fantasy genre, given the studio and the title of the film. It features traditional animation, a fairy tale narrative, and stock characters such as a princess, a wicked stepmother and a handsome prince. The film also features many conventions associated with the musical, with several set piece performances and extravagant *mise en scène* – a trope clearly associated with Disney fantasies. Yet the film goes further in an attempt to broaden its target audience by skewing the narrative towards the romantic comedy, setting it in a glamorous New York setting recognizable from so many other romantic comedies and constructing a modern romantic narrative which clashes with the Disney tradition. Ultimately,

49

the film complies with all the expectations of classical narrative cinema – the linear narrative, closure, spectacle alongside plot progression and conventional discourses around romance, human relationships and social order. The film plays with the genre building blocks so that, even though it could be categorized as fantasy, it also references comedy and the musical, although in an ironic way which enables it to extend its appeal.

Genre and ideology

Genre criticism was not merely concerned with the outer form of a film and the issue as to whether its superficial qualities fitted with the iconography of a specific genre. Theorists were interested in how the extrinsic nature of a genre was used to articulate specific themes and issues which could be argued to have a sociocultural dimension. Bazin had been interested in exploring the myth that lay at the heart of the western, attempting to explain how the formal qualities of the genre evoked a timeless theme of the fight against evil, with the agents of civilization – cowboys – struggling to overcome the forces of evil (generally the Native Americans in the 'classic' form of the genre). He believed that this fundamental myth helped to explain the global appeal of the genre.

Studies regarding the ideology of genre tended to argue that genres worked to support and convey certain sociocultural values. At one extreme the Marxist viewpoint argued that Hollywood genre films were part of the larger ideological apparatus of the state, helping to support capitalist values and beliefs. Other theorists developed the concept of the myth and explored the idea that genre films convey deeply held beliefs and desires, acting as a collective 'ritualisation of . . . ideals, the celebration of temporarily resolved social and cultural conflicts, and the concealment of disturbing cultural conflicts behind the guise of entertainment' (Schatz, 1986, p97). Schatz argued that all genre films could be allocated to one of two overall genre groupings – the 'genre of order' (the western, gangster and science fiction) and the 'genre of integration' (musicals, comedies, melodramas; Schatz, 1981). He argued that each grouping shared common hero types, themes, narratives and settings, dealing with common themes and ideologies. Schatz provided an interesting approach to genre, which explored the common themes that are submerged by very different iconographies. For example, the western and science fiction inhabit very different kinds of *mise en scène*, yet both tend to be dominated by male characters, featuring violent action and gaining resolution through death. Both of these genres tend to look towards the hero to resolve society's problems and to restore order, prioritizing a macho code of behaviour.

Increasingly, genre studies considered the extent to which genre films reflected the social, economic and political context of production. The romantic comedy is one genre where the treatment of the central narrative can be related to the wider context. The screwball comedies of the 1930s offered escapism from the harsh realities of the Depression, the narratives offering intensity, energy and fun, with a happy ending for the couple. Films such as *It Happened One Night* (1934) and *Bringing up Baby* (1938) had a clear central message that love is the route to happiness – money is not everything – as the heroines gladly exchange their lives of privilege for a life in the ordinary world. The heroines in both of these films are represented as spoilt and arrogant in an indictment of the effect of wealth; they both have to learn a difficult lesson in order to be worthy of the 'right man'. A different position regarding the screwball comedy would argue that it worked to reinforce traditional gender roles, with the female lead characters in both films needing to be subdued and yoked to a male partner in order to restore order and stability. Both female characters have to be humbled and submit to their 'husbands' in order to attain happiness. In this respect, the screwball sub-genre is typical of the wider genre in promoting heterosexuality and marriage as the foundation of a healthy and happy society.

The different approaches to considering the ideological function of genre were endemic of the move away from merely placing the film within a genre, and tended to reflect thinking about the role of the audience and the wider cultural framework for popular film. The Marxist viewpoint implied a passive audience, who are being indoctrinated by genre texts. The concept concerning the mythic force of genre, on the other hand, presupposes an active audience who choose to watch a film for certain pleasures and reassurances, even to explore and release emotions in contrast to their everyday lives. In this respect, genre films could be considered to offer cathartic pleasures in a ritualized form packaged within a specific genre.

Taking genre further

The debates over genre theory have formed a vital part of the development of film studies' critical landscape, having opened up popular cinema for analysis and endeavoured to liberate the subject from the narrow scrutiny circumscribed by auteur theory. Genre theory has evolved and revised itself constantly, and has resulted in many interesting new perspectives for the academic study of film. It has grown from being an attempt to label by extending its remit to encompass the industrial and audience contexts, mapping the sociocultural and ideological environment.

Some theorists argue that cinema has entered a post-generic mode, proclaiming the death of genre. This is indicative of a heightened awareness of the popularity of films which appear to defy generic classification, being multigeneric. The *Pirates of the Caribbean* series is typical in being a hybrid of costume drama, fantasy, action/adventure and comedy. These 'event movies' – as contemporary blockbusters have been christened – are still the exception, as the majority of Hollywood products have clear genre identities.

There is also a greater interest in the genre system outside Hollywood with a critical awareness of genres which are characteristic of national cinemas, such as the Bollywood musical. Increasingly, cinema has been considered on a transnational basis in this respect, as genres outside the realm of Hollywood have actually fed back into and renewed Hollywood genres. For example, Japanese horror – such as *The Ring* and *Grudge* series – have influenced Hollywood, with English language remakes having a subsequent effect on the nature of the Hollywood horror genre. Just as the Hollywood genre system has its own context in terms of history, industry and audience, other national cinemas have been recognized as having their own traditions and contexts in terms of genre.

Contemporary genre studies has seen a greater emphasis on inter-textuality and has moved away from considering the film in isolation towards an exploration of how the film is situated *vis à vis* other films of the same genre and beyond. This approach sees genre as schema and exploring how the spectator's experience is a process of making sense through references to prior film experience. The spectator knows what to expect in terms of generic tropes and yet is able to appreciate departures and generic innovation. In this respect, there can be no film which does not have some kind of generic imprint, whether it be popular Hollywood cinema or not; in the words of Jacques Derrida (1981, p61): 'a text cannot belong to no genre, it cannot be without . . . a genre. Every text participates in one or several genres, there is no genre-less text.'

Summary

- The contemporary study of genre is an intrinsic part of film studies; much like the genres themselves, the theory is constantly evolving and responding to other debates and theories.

- Genre is dynamic and a constant process; it is not fixed.
- Despite genre theory being developed to compensate for the perceived elitism or dominance of auteur theory, the concept of 'genre films' is mainly associated with Hollywood popular cinema and is often used to indicate inferiority of such product.
- Genre theory can be a useful approach in exploring film form and dynamics, yet needs to consider wider contextual factors.
- Genre is a context for understanding the 'meaning' and dynamics of a film text.

References and further reading

Bazin, A. (1971) *What is Cinema?*, University of California Press, Berkeley, CA

Bell, J. (2012) 'La Régle du Jeu', *Sight and Sound*, September: p51.

Derrida, J. (1981) 'The law of genre', in W. J. T. Mitchell (ed) *On Narrative*, University of Chicago Press, Chicago, IL

Hutchby, P. (1995) 'Genre theory and criticism', in J. A. Hollows (ed) *Approaches to Popular Film*, Manchester University Press, Manchester, UK, p61

Kutner, C. J. (2006) 'Beyond the Golden Age', *Bright Lights Film Journal*, November, http://www.brightlightsfilm.com/54/noirgolden.php

Maltby, R. (2003) *Hollywood Cinema*, Blackwell, Malden, MA

Matthews, P. (2012) 'Vertigo', *Sight and Sound*, September: pp54–5.

Neale, S. (1980) *Genre*, British Film Institute, London

— (1990) 'Questions of genre', *Screen*, vol 31, no 1, pp35–57

Schatz, T. (1981) *Hollywood Genres*, McGraw Hill, New York, NY

— (1986) 'Hollywood genres: Formulas, filmmaking, and the studio system', in B. K. Grant (ed.) *Film Genre Reader*, University of Texas Press, Austin, TX

Stam, R. (2000) *Film Theory: An Introduction*, Blackwell, Malden, MA

Tudor, A. (1989) *Monsters and Mad Scientists: A Cultural History of the Horror Movie*, Blackwell, Oxford

Wright, W. (1975) *Sixguns and Society*, University of California Press, Berkeley, CA

If you wish to extend your knowledge of genre further, a good place to start would be Steve Neale's *Genre and Hollywood* (Routledge, 2000). Another useful source is the Peter Hutchings' chapter 'Genre theory and criticism' in *Approaches to Popular Film*, edited by Joanne Hollows and Mark Jancovitch (Manchester University Press, 1995).

5

Competing Approaches

Screen Theory

In this chapter we will consider:

- What is screen theory?
- Is cinema inherently ideological?
- How is meaning produced through the relationship between text and spectator?
- How has psychoanalysis been applied to cinema?

The study of film can seem quite daunting once you realize the extraordinary complexity and diversity of film theory. Much of film theory draws on other academic disciplines, and can seem require an understanding of areas of knowledge which can be obscure and demanding. This is certainly true of screen theory – an overarching name for a range of important theoretical developments which have had a significant impact upon the development of the academic study of film. This chapter aims to give an overview of the key aspects of screen theory, which have come to have a profound effect on how we study film. Inevitably, it is an extremely reductive account, and you would be advised to undertake further reading to develop a fuller understanding of the theories.

Where did screen theory come from?

In order to understand the academic upheaval which led to screen theory, it is useful to contemplate the wider social context. The late 1960s witnessed student revolt, with unrest spreading across Europe and America. A crisis point for the western world occurred in May 1968, with the student riots in France spurred on by the anti-authoritarian 'New Left' who had embraced a new era of socialism, influenced by feminism and anti-colonialism. In effect, 1968 was a turning point for western culture, with widespread consequences, not least of which was the impact upon academia. Marxist ideology gained popular appeal among elements of the intelligentsia, in tune with a resounding rejection of the status quo in terms of canons and established critical thinking. The age demanded a questioning of what had come before – in particular, a critical awareness of how the 'masses' were subject to the ideological potential of film and popular culture.

Of course, as with any changes in the critical climate, the emergence of so-called 'screen theory' was not an overnight phenomenon, and there were theorists who had developed similar lines of thinking beforehand. Nevertheless, there was a discernible impact upon the theoretical landscape at this time, and certain key figures led the debate. Comolli and Narboni set the tone in 1969 in an editorial for *Cahiers du Cinema* – 'Cinema/ideology/criticism' – calling for a politically engaged criticism which embraced the ideological aspects of cinema at every level. This call to arms encapsulated the radical tone, which aimed to overhaul film studies, and academia as a whole. Central to this was the move from the study of meaning, as embodied in the text, to the question of how meaning is created through the meeting of text and spectator. The British cinema journal *Screen* was to become the most important theoretical journal of the visual arts in the UK by embracing key thinking around ideology, subjectivity, semiotics, psychoanalysis and Marxism. In particular, it sought to develop a politicized theory of film which explored the role of cinema in perpetuating the dominant ideology.

Film theory during the 1970s was dominated by the rejection of approaches based on authorship and aesthetics, instead studying the theories of Roland Barthes, Louis Althusser, Jean-Louis Baudry and Christian Metz, among others. *Screen* took a leading role in publishing some of the key arguments and contributions to the theoretical debate. As a consequence it influenced the direction of film studies at a critical time, when the subject was starting to become established within universities. Screen theory took its name from the journal, yet actually encompasses a diverse group of theoretical approaches. What did link these approaches, though, was the rejection of the discrete study of film, whether by genre, authorship or stars, in favour of a theory which analysed the structure of cinema itself.

Screen's theoretical impulse was heavily indebted to the structuralist movement – a broad philosophical and methodological approach which argued that subjectivity was dependent upon pre-existing social structures, such as language, family and cultural frameworks, such as education, law and order, and religion.

Film as text: Ideology and cinema

The New Left counterculture of the later 1960s was characterized by a rejection of the establishment, and an accompanying suspicion of the 'status quo' throughout society. This was reflected in a film theory which started to probe the ideological dimensions of film texts, seeing mainstream film merely as a tool with which society could continue to perpetuate the inherent inequal-ities and injustices perceived as being fundamental to western capitalist structures.

Marxist theorists such as Althusser argued that the individual is effectively conditioned by the dominant class to believe that they are 'free', and therefore continue to accept their position, serving the interests of the powerful few. The theory regards cinema as part of the cultural machinery which serves to reproduce this 'bourgeois ideology', working alongside other 'ideological state apparatuses' (a term coined by Althusser) such as schools, the church, families and other cultural agencies to help maintain the hierarchies and stability of capitalist societies.

This radical questioning of the role of popular culture had a profound impact upon film theory, leading to an emphasis on approaching film as a text which is inscribed with a clear ideology, designed to position the spectator as a 'subject', to be manipulated and positioned by the bourgeoisie. For theorists such as Colin MacCabe this positioning worked on a series of levels – for example, the structures of film language, editing and camerawork are used to position the spectator within the text. Likewise, the spectator is positioned by the narrative structure of the film, being aligned with specific characters and gratified by the escapism of the classic narrative structure. The exercise of film criticism is transformed into an investigation into the ideological nature of the text, central to the development of psychoanalytic and feminist film theory during the 1970s.

This new consciousness of the ideological dimension of cinema necessitated a revision of the concept of 'realism' within film. Realism had continued to be at the heart of critical debates since the beginnings of film criticism, yet the new theory suggested that the 'realism' of films positioned the spectator to accept the values and ideology of the narrative as 'natural' and 'common sense'. The film theory of the 1970s argued that the general consensus that cinema captured reality facilitated its ideological function in reinforcing socially dominant values and ideas. One response to this was to argue that a new cinema was needed, the objective of which would be to politically enlighten the spectator by deliberately going against realist conventions, and heighten their awareness of their subjectivity regarding the powerful elite. This radical approach was not new as it echoed the political sense of mission behind Russian formalist cinema, which had experimented with anti-realist techniques in order to raise the consciousness of the spectator and deliver powerful political messages.

The ideal form for this new cinema would be avant-garde film, which seeks to actively engage the spectator by drawing attention to film form, rather than seeking to make it 'invisible' in the mode of classical realist cinema. Essentially, screen theory reduced cinema to a polarized opposition between the innately conservative nature of popular cinema and the ideological potential offered by the avant-garde, which can challenge the spectator's assumptions and beliefs regarding culture and society. This approach was complicated by identifying examples of popular cinema which appeared to support the dominant ideology, yet were distinguished by inherent contradictions and tensions within the text. This allowed film theorists some leeway within which to recognize the achievements of certain auteurs who work within mainstream cinema, such as John Ford and Alfred Hitchcock.

Psychoanalysis and film theory

The film theory of the 1970s served to re-orient film criticism by placing the spectator at the centre of the critical approach, developing a theory of subjectivity. In foregrounding the ideological dimensions of film, Marxist critics envisaged a spectator who is the subject of the film text, stimulating subsequent academic debate regarding the implicit passivity of the audience in this formulation of the cinema experience. Film theory was further radicalized by the impact of psychoanalytical theory, forming new modes of thinking about film which have continued to have a fundamental impact upon the subject.

The relationship between psychoanalysis and cinema is complex, both having had a profound effect on the twentieth century since their origins at the end of the previous century. Cinema has continued to be influenced by psychoanalytical theory, with narratives structured around desire and the metaphorical resonance of cinema as a 'dream factory' offering escapism and diversion. Barbara Creed goes further in claiming that cinema may well have influenced psychoanalysis itself: 'Not only did Freud draw on cinematic terms to describe his theories, as in "screen memories", but a number of his key ideas were developed in visual terms' (Creed, 1998, p77). The theories of Freud and Lacan were to be most influential regarding film theory of the 1970s.

Film theorists developed a critical landscape which was based on Freud's theories regarding the unconscious, sexuality and subjectivity in order to explore the relationship between the film text and the spectator. This perspective sees the film as a text which projects fantasies and desires, drawing on the realms of the unconscious in appealing to the spectator. Critics explored film texts for evidence of repressed desires, the workings of the unconscious and narratives which conformed to the Oedipal trajectory. For the theorist of the 1970s, Lacan's theories were to offer a new impetus to psychoanalytic film theory, specifically Lacan's 'mirror stage' theory.

Lacan's concept of the mirror stage responds to Freud's theories concerning the development of the child's sense of self. Lacan argued that the child goes through a sequence of stages, the mirror stage being when the child sees itself as complete, yet believes itself more adult and perfect than it really is. It is a moment of revelation – and joy – but also of misrecognition, as the child is mistaken. The mirror stage is thus a moment in which the self is split between recognition and misrecognition.

For theorists such as Jean-Louis Baudry this provides the basis for an approach to cinema which explains the processes of identification underlying the viewing experience. The context of the viewing experience – the darkened room, the power of the projector and screen – reconstructs the mirror stage for the spectator, encouraging them to experience transcendence once more. We regress willingly to the mirror stage of childhood, relating to the idealized self who is projected in the mirror/screen in a moment of repeated recognition/ misrecognition. We recognize ourselves in characters on the screen, but simultaneously relating to an idealized self, who is perhaps greater in being more than we can ever be: more perfect, more desirable, braver.

Baudry applied Lacan's mirror stage theory in analysing the institution of cinema. For him, cinema is ideological in contriving to construct a sense of transcendence and unity within the spectator, which is effectively a state of misrecognition. Cinema creates an impression of realism, seemingly placing the spectator at the centre of the viewing experience through the use of filmic devices such as continuity editing and reassuring narratives which resolve conflicts and restore harmony. For Baudry, cinema is an apparatus which encourages a state of regression and a false sense of control and unity for the spectator, harnessing our desires in the consensual reproduction of the dominant ideology: we welcome the chance to embrace and re-enact the mirror stage. It is an apparatus which works alongside other sociocultural entities, such as the church, in perpetuating the values and beliefs ingrained in society.

This line of psychoanalytic theory regards the ideological potential of film as particularly powerful due to the nature of the viewing experience itself: the spectator is passive, a subject to be manipulated by the realism of the film text, immobile within the darkened womb-like space of the cinema and away from the pressures of the real world. Robert Stam describes this as 'a kind of double whammy . . . extremely strong visual and auditory stimuli inundate us at a moment when we are predisposed toward passive reception and narcissistic self-absorption' (Stam, 2000, p163). The re-experiencing of the mirror stage offered by cinema provides a moment of unity and escape – a return to the transcendent experience of power and control – which provides relief from the divided self who is perpetually experiencing a state of loss and a corresponding desire for completeness.

Christian Metz was to further develop this 'apparatus theory', arguing that 'the cinematic institution is not just the cinema industry . . . it is also the mental machinery – another industry – which spectators "accustomed to the cinema" have internalized historically and which has adapted them to the consumption of films' (Metz, 1982, p8). Central to this psychoanalytic film criticism is the concern with how the spectator is subjectified in the viewing experience by the cinema apparatus. For Metz, the relationship between the spectator and the screen is voyeuristic, structured around the experience of seeing without being seen, and the illicit pleasures created by this sense of power and privilege. The spectator is essentially a peeping Tom who is given intimate access to another world which cannot look back.

Metz referred to cinema as the 'imaginary signifier', arguing that it works to make present what is absent. The projected images merely signify events which happened elsewhere, at another time. Metz argued that the spectator does not identify with what it sees on the screen but is aware that it is imaginary, adding to the sense of distance which enshrouds the voyeuristic act of spectatorship. He also drew on Lacan's theories in exploring the fetishistic nature of the representation of women in film. Fetishism – endowing objects with magical and erotic powers – is seen to motivate the 'over-investment' in images of fragmented parts of the female form, used to signify the erotic potential of the whole. This explains the repeated shots of legs, lips and even items of female clothing which hold an erotic charge for the spectator.

Metz and Baudry led the way in developing a psychoanalytic film theory in the 1970s, opening up an energetic debate among film academics, as their ideas were elaborated, rejected and modified (even by themselves). This new film theory was also to be the catalyst for feminist film theory.

Feminist film theory

Sexuality and desire was fundamental to psychoanalytical film theory, drawing heavily on the ideas of Freud and Lacan, particularly the arguments around the importance of sexuality in the formation of subjectivity. Nevertheless, feminist film theorists took issue with theory which presupposed a male spectator, foregrounding male desires and pleasures – a patriarchal film theory which excludes the female spectator. Laura Mulvey took on the debate in 1975 with her influential article published in *Screen* 'Visual pleasure and narrative cinema', appropriating psychoanalytic theory to give a feminist perspective.

Mulvey's essay was a call to action, demanding a new cinema which would provoke thought, rather than pleasure, by breaking away from dominant cinematic practices in favour of a feminist film form. The basis for this radical position was her argument that classical narrative cinema was centred on a gendered perspective, which offered the woman as an objectified source of pleasure, at the mercy of the 'male gaze'. For Mulvey, film form simply replicates and reinforces the gender imbalances within the film industry, and society as a whole. Her theoretical standpoint can be seen to be analogous to Baudry's apparatus theory in considering the ideological effect of the cinematic apparatus.

Mulvey based her arguments on aspects of psychoanalytical theory – in particular, voyeurism, fetishism and identification. She argued that mainstream cinema is structured around three types of 'gaze': the gaze of the camera, the looks between characters and the spectator's gaze. The spectator is inevitably positioned to identify with the dominant gaze of the male protagonist, and thus is aligned with the male viewpoint throughout the narrative. Mulvey's theory rests on a system of interpellation – considering how the spectator is positioned by the film text – which suggests that mainstream cinema determines a fixed viewing position which is essentially patriarchal, reflecting the embedded power structures of society as a whole. Classical narrative conventions demand an active male protagonist and a correspondingly passive female counterpart, who is there to be looked at but does not play an active role in the narrative.

Mulvey's feminist reading of the dynamics of film language asserted that the gaze is constructed through point of view, editing and framing of the shot. The viewing process is centred on the pleasure of seeing – scopophilia – which positions the woman as the object of the gaze. By making the woman the object of pleasurable viewing, she is rendered passive and objectified for sexual pleasure. Mulvey asserted that film narratives could be voyeuristic yet fused with sadistic impulses, giving the example of film noir, where the *femme fatale* is punished or has to undergo the process of redemption in order to defuse their threat. Film could also be fetishistic, as in the example of Sternburg, where the film narrative is paused to display the spectacle of close-ups of the female form, which are endowed with erotic magical power.

So if mainstream cinema is determined by patriarchal structures, for the pleasure of the male spectator, then what of the female spectator? This was a central concern for subsequent interventions in feminist film theory, and not least from Mulvey herself. She was to elaborate upon her theory, suggesting that the female spectator may identify with the dominant viewpoint of the male protagonist, sublimating her own sexual identity or, conversely, relating to the passive female object of the gaze. This was certainly seen to be a rather unsatisfactory aspect of Mulvey's initial position, implying a female audience in a perpetual state of compromise, being forced to take a subordinate position.

Mulvey argued in favour of an oppositional cinema, which liberated the spectator from the male gaze that had tied them into the patriarchal ideologies of mainstream cinema. As a film-maker, she put her theory into practice by working towards a feminist cinema which breaks the codes and denies narrative pleasure. For her, as with other politically engaged film-makers of the era, the way forward was avant-garde cinema: a cinema which deliberately broke the rules in order to challenge the spectator and engage them politically.

The screen legacy

In effect, *Screen* was to take the academic discipline of film studies by the scruff of its neck and give it a good shaking at an important moment in its development, as it started to become established within higher education. It set out to delineate an overarching theory of film studies, but ultimately failed in this, although succeeding in being the catalyst and channel for theoretical debates which were to have a lasting influence on the subject. Mulvey's essay 'Visual pleasure and narrative cinema' was to have a seismic impact upon feminist film theory, audience theory and the emergence of cultural studies. *Screen* set the agenda for film and media studies, with many of its associates going on to take university posts.

Summary

- Ideology has become integral to film studies, as we consider how a film text works in terms of political and ideological beliefs.
- Psychoanalytical film theory has informed subsequent theory regarding how the spectator watches the film text and the pleasures of cinema.
- Feminist film theory integrated the ideological and psychoanalytical approach, and consequently stimulated debates around gender, film and audience.
- Film can be considered an inherently political subject.

References and further reading

Creed, B. (1998) 'Film and psychoanalysis', in J. Hill and P. Church Gibson (ed) *The Oxford Guide to Film Studies*, Oxford University Press, Oxford, pp77–90

Maltby, R. (2003) *Hollywood Cinema*, Blackwell, Malden, MA

Metz, C. (1982) *The Imaginary Signifier: Psychoanalysis and the Cinema*, Indiana University Press, Bloomington, IN

Mulvey, L. (1975) 'Visual pleasure and narrative cinema', *Screen*, vol 16, no 3, pp6–18

Stam, R. (2000) *Film Theory: An Introduction*, Blackwell, Malden, MA

Mark Jancovitch's chapter on screen theory in *Approaches to Popular Film*, edited by Joanne Hollows and Mark Jancovitch (Manchester University Press, 1995), goes into much greater detail about the theoretical complexity of screen theory.

PART III

STUDYING THE FILM TEXT

6

Reading a Film

In this chapter we will consider:

- How do we read a film?
- What are the tools available to interrogate film?
- What is meant by film language?
- Why is film style important?

The starting point for any film course is to introduce students to the fundamentals of the film text, analysing the composition of the moving image in order to develop an understanding of how film works to create meaning. This is the foundation of any further study of film, developing an appreciation of style and meaning before going on to address the array of topics, academic debates and creative options which constitute a typical film course. Film 'language' is the essence of the study of film, the understanding of which should illuminate the working of film, giving you the tools to appreciate, understand and respond to the text. Studying film is not merely a naming of parts – identifying a particular camera technique or transition, for example – but is more about developing an appreciation of the subtleties and nuances of aspects of film style, and the significance of creative choices in the making of a film text.

The elements of film language

The study of the fundamental essence of film will tend to isolate a range of filmic features, which constitute what is often referred to as film language. These features form the currency of film studies, namely: cinematography, editing, sound, *mise en scène* and performance. The study of each of these elements encompasses an appreciation of the diverse stylistic choices made during the film-making process, requiring the knowledge of a specialist vocabulary in order to specify a particular technique or effect, and opening up an appreciation of the stylistic features of particular cinemas, periods in the history of film, genres and auteurs. In short, the study of film language is a gateway to a broader and more informed knowledge of film as a whole.

For example, a film such as Howard Hawks's *Bringing up Baby* (1938) may be used as a text to illustrate performance style, perhaps studying the central performance of Katharine Hepburn. Hepburn's performance is distinguished by its fast pace in terms of movement and speech, with witty repartee and insistent driving patter. She strides into the centre of the frame and demonstrates athletic prowess, whether it be in throwing peanuts up into the air and catching them in her mouth or gamely tackling a wild leopard. This performance style defines Hepburn's film persona – a trouser-wearing, feisty, opinionated modern girl from a wealthy liberal family – which informs her illustrious film career. Yet it also defines the genre, in her performance as the archetypal 'fast-talking dame' of the screwball comedy; furthermore it is a performance style which defines an era, and the impact of technological innovation: the fast-paced dialogue characterized Hollywood cinema in the early years of sound. Another possible angle on this aspect of film language could address the extent to which this performance style and characterization defines the work of the director, Howard Hawks, whose female leads tended to be strong, intelligent and heroic.

The analysis of film language is the basis of informed interrogation of the film text, which may focus on one particular aspect of the moving image, yet is more likely to integrate the consideration of all elements. The total effect of film is created by the complex relationship between all of these elements, which is a dynamic process, as is the nature of the moving image. A film text, as a whole, may have certain distinguishing stylistic elements, as with the example of performance in *Bringing up Baby*; but within an individual scene there will be significant shifts in lighting, costume or camerawork which contribute to the creation of meaning. In this respect, film language can be considered on a macro level – in broad terms – yet needs to be interrogated on a micro level, within a single shot, scene or sequence. A full understanding of film language needs to appreciate the interplay between all of its elements, for the meaning of each is inflected by its relationship with others. Performance cannot be studied in isolation, as it is clearly created by the interplay of camerawork, editing, lighting, sound, costume and other aspects of *mise en scène*.

What is film style?

The ability to respond to film style is a question of developing film literacy, developing a sensitivity to the elements of film language, and being able to articulate this response. There is a paradox at the heart of this: in watching a film we are saturated with fast-moving imagery and densely textured soundscapes which our minds are able to process and comprehend instantaneously, yet the skill of developing an informed, sensitive critical response demands that we pause the flow of imagery and sound in order to capture the workings and essence of film style. John Gibbs and Douglas Pye assert that style 'is a web, a network, a texture, a pattern, or, more mechanistically, a system', which results from the decision-making process undertaken by the film-maker (Gibbs and Pye, 2005, p11). The consideration of the decisions made in selecting formal techniques also needs to take into consideration the broader context of the film's production: the industrial and social context which shapes the film-making process. The ability to respond meaningfully to film style is integral to the process of interrogating the film text, yet will also enhance your ability to form a critical response.

From previous chapters, you will now appreciate how the discipline of film studies has struggled to find its identity and assert its academic credentials as it has matured as a subject. Inevitably, this has involved plenty of academic schisms, and the issue of film style has certainly not been exempt from this. The academic Geoffrey Nowell-Smith points out that the problem of film meaning has been a central concern of film theorists since the 1920s, along with the problem of representation (Nowell-Smith, 2000). The two issues are clearly connected in terms of how film uses form to represent the world, and how this representation creates meaning. The theoretical debate around these issues has evolved over time, in very broad terms, from an early concern with the aesthetics of film, developing into the critical dialogue between the realists and the formalists, and the later impetus towards a theoretical framework for analysis of film form using semiotic analysis. The current era, on the other hand, has witnessed a renewed interest in aesthetics within a discipline which harnesses a range of theoretical perspectives.

What is film?

It may be helpful to consider the difference between 'film' and 'cinema'. The theorist Christian Metz suggests that cinema is the film-making institution, encompassing production, distribution, exhibition and film viewing. The film is the text which is the product of the cinema industry; it is essentially a form of narrative which utilizes visual and aural imagery to engage a spectator. On the most rudimentary level, the basic constituents of the film are the shot and the cut, with the film coming into being with the placing of shots in relation to each other in order to create meaning.

What is film language?

So, to what extent can film be compared to a language? Certainly, the concept of a language implies a system of communication, using recognizable signs to convey meaning. In this respect, film could be argued to operate as a language, combining elements of visual and aural imagery to communicate meaning to the spectator. When analysing film extracts we are examining how these 'signs' have been combined to create meaning, as the basis of our interrogation of the film text. But really the similarity finishes there, as film does not have the same defined units of meaning equivalent to the words of any language. Film does not have a prescribed grammar in terms of rules and systems governing composition. Of course, there are certain recognizable conventions which we expect of narrative film, such as continuity editing, which assist in creating meaning and facilitating our engagement with the film text.

Formalist film theory

The response to the very earliest films tended to dwell on the realism of the images and the novelty of the moving image in the 'cinema of attractions'. The limited critical response to early film appraised the form in terms of its veracity and the phenomenon of movement within the frame, whether it be the apocryphal accounts of the shocked audience reaction to the train bearing down on them in the Lumière brothers' *L'Arrivée d'un Train à la Ciotat* (1895) or the movement of the leaves in the background which fascinated the audience watching *Le Repas (de Bébé)* (1895).

The idea of film as language was prevalent in the silent era, in response to its ability to convey meaning without words (with the exception of inter-titles). Early critics compared cinema to an art form, such as painting, poetry or sculpture, in terms its ability to create meaning through movement and rhythm, and the intensity of its effect on the spectator. There was a critical impetus to validate cinema as an art form, seeing the value of 'pure' cinema in terms of how it renders an event 'different to reality', rather than merely seeking to reproduce reality. Critics sought to define the essence of cinema: what were its unique distinguishing elements which could be cited in evaluating its status as an art form? The French director Abel Gance described cinema as 'music of light', whilst elsewhere it was compared to music, being a form of visual symphony (Perkins 1993: 14–15). Many of these early theorists were fascinated by the aesthetics of cinema, and the potential of the image and the edit to render a version of reality which becomes an artistic statement, in effect *more* than a simple reproduction of reality. This concern with aesthetics entails a study of film for its own sake, not for the sake of considering a wider concept, theory or social purpose. The aesthetic experience presupposes contemplation of an artwork, giving film an enhanced status in terms of having greater value than a mere form of mass entertainment.

These early theorists initiated a debate which laid the foundations for the study of film. This formalist film theory believed that film is an art form which transcends realism. The claims that cinema was an art form led inevitably towards a film hierarchy in terms of artistic merit. The greatest films were those that conveyed an artistic vision, such as the German expressionist film *The Cabinet of Dr Caligari* (1920), acclaimed for its imagination and creativity, with its distinctively stylized set design, cinematography and performance style. Theorists argued that lesser examples of the form merely sought to reproduce reality as accurately as possible, subjugating form and creativity to realism. They set out to prove that film-making was not a craft form, where technology can be used to reproduce reality, but was an art form, where the techniques and choices employed by the film-maker had the potential to render the moving image meaningful and expressive.

This emphasis on aesthetics prompted critical reflection as to the composition of the shot, and how camerawork and organization of the image could be made expressive, rather than merely striving for realism. The claim of film to be an art form was reinforced by critical attention to camera angles and composition, believing that all the elements of the shot should 'be employed expressively' with 'the overt use of photographic devices of selection and distortion as a means of commenting upon objects and events', according to film scholar V. F. Perkins (1993, p18). By extension, it is uncinematic if the camera is used to record reality, with no attempt at expressivity.

A significant body of opinion held that montage (as in the French word for editing, rather than a specific style of editing) is what distinguished film as art, allowing the film-maker to control time and space, with the creative possibilities of the edit. The Hungarian critic Bela Balazs proclaimed that montage was 'the mobile architecture of the film's picture material . . . a specific, new creative art' (Balazs, 1952, p46). The possibilities of the edit were explored during the era of silent film, when film-makers rapidly developed sophisticated use of editing to develop narrative and involve the audience. The Soviet formalist film-makers embraced the creative potential of the edit, seeing its potential in terms of using the juxtaposition of certain shots to create powerful meanings, challenging and energizing the spectator as the experience of watching the film becomes a dynamic experience. The Russian director V. I. Pudovkin pronounced that 'Editing is the language of the film director. Just as in living speech, so, one may say, in editing: there is a word – the piece of exposed film, the image; a phrase – the combination of these pieces' (Pudovkin, 1958, p100).

The Soviet formalists were not only concerned with the aesthetics of montage, seeing it as a tool which had ideological potential in terms of actively involving the spectator in making meaning. The film-maker and theorist Sergei Eisenstein put his ideas into practice in films such as *Battleship Potemkin* (1925); montage editing is used in the celebrated Odessa steps sequence to shock the spectator into sympathy with the various hapless victims of the Tzarist troops, juxtaposing imagery of the military might in contrast with various shots of the victims, particularly the helpless baby whose pram hurtles down the steps after the murder of the mother. The elements of film-making are harnessed for a purpose beyond conveying an artistic vision or being contemplated for their own worth in the work of the Soviet formalists. The film has an ideological agenda and seeks to engage the spectator by the provocative use of montage in this particular sequence. Eisenstein believed that the shot was merely the raw material for the film-maker; the editing process constructs meaning by juxtaposition of shots.

Mise en scène and the realistic aesthetic

The introduction of sound cinema during the late 1920s posed an immense challenge to some theorists. Sound was regarded with great suspicion, seen as detracting from the potential of film as a visual art form, moving it more towards the technical replication of reality. The fear was that cinema would become a means of reproducing the theatre, rather than an art form which utilized the visual potential of the shot and the edit. Much of the uneasiness concerning the introduction of sound rested on an assumption that realism and art could not coexist within cinema.

The formalist position was in complete opposition to a significant body of opinion that argued that the essence of cinema was its ability to replicate real life. The realists believed that cinema had the ability to capture the truth of reality, offering a credibility which is absent in other art forms in terms of being able to record objectively, without the creative interference of the artist. French critic and theorist André Bazin was the figurehead for the realists, believing in 'the myth of total cinema' in terms of being 'a total and complete representation of reality . . . the reconstruction of a perfect illusion of the outside world in sound, color, and relief' (Bazin, 1967, p20).

The realist aesthetic entailed a rethinking of the elements of film in order to achieve the sense of realism, dispensing with the overt stylization and expressiveness which were esteemed by the formalists. The overall tendency was very much to minimize a sense of artistic intervention, to render the film image as natural and *un*constructed as is possible given the essential constructed nature of film. A true artist must be able to select aspects of reality which perfectly summarize the complexity of the whole for the spectator. Perkins argues that Bazin's concept of cinema rests on a different concept of the film-maker as artist, in which the film-maker 'is acutely aware of the primary and primitive powers of the bare image . . . it takes artistry . . . to reveal significance through the unadorned image' (Perkins, 1993, pp168–169). A single shot should be able to evoke the complexity of experience.

For Bazin, the key to realism was the long take, deep focus and *mise en scène*. His stance was the complete opposite to the formalists, seeing the single shot as the essence of cinema. The shot should be composed as a work of art in itself, using lighting, staging, deep focus and movement to create a sense of uninterrupted wholeness, which invites the spectator into the frame and allows ownership of the image in terms of the gaze being liberated rather than controlled by the film-maker. This is in contrast to the tightly controlled montage of Russian formalism, where no one shot is deemed worthy in itself, meaning being created by the juxtaposition of shots; the spectator is owned by the film-maker, manipulated by creative intervention and manipulation.

Mise en scène is central to Bazin's concept of cinema, and was to become extremely influential in the development of film theory in the pages of the French film journal *Cahiers du Cinema* (partly founded by Bazin) and the British journal *Movie*. The analysis of *mise en scène* – composition, lighting, movement, performance and colour – allowed for the study of the individual elements of the film, providing a basis for academic study which distinguished it from other art forms (although Bazin was very influenced by art). *Mise en scène* became key to developing an understanding of narrative and the impact upon the spectator. Moreover, in conjunction with auteur theory, it became a way of distinguishing the work of specific 'artists' within cinema, illuminating their distinctive use of *mise en scène* in defining individual style.

Much as with the formalist position, the arguments for a realist cinema could be partially traced to a wider political context. The realist aesthetic argued for a democratic cinema, which held a mirror to the world, representing the ordinary and the real, which have value in themselves. Realism was endowed with greater political urgency in the 1940s, inspiring and inspired by the Italian neo-realists, whose films recorded the plight of ordinary Italians in the wake of the war, casting non-professional actors and structuring narratives around the seemingly banal, such as the theft of a bicycle in Vittorio de Sica's *Bicycle Thieves* (1948) or the desperation of a poverty-stricken pensioner in de Sica's *Umberto D* (1952). These films were largely filmed on location, their veracity being enhanced by the realism of the settings and the use of available light, although this was largely a necessity due to financial constraints and the debilitated state of the cinema industry in the wake of the war.

Semiology

It is unsurprising that the 1970s witnessed the next seismic reappraisal of textual analysis, led by the publication of a special edition of the British journal *Screen* in 1973, which was devoted to the work of theorist Christian Metz and cinema semiotics. Metz set out to apply linguistic structures to cinema in order to establish whether film was a language, and whether linguistic methods could develop our understanding of how film creates meaning. At the heart of this approach was the concept of signification, arguing that a language is composed of signifiers which relate to what is signified. The problem posed by film is that signifiers such as a particular camera shot, a prop or use of colour can have many possible meanings, unlike language, where the possible meanings conveyed by a word are finite. Metz argued that cinema worked as a composite artistic language, using a web of codes and systems to create meaning. These codes are recognizable rules which are associated with particular meanings, including technical codes (filmic techniques such as camerawork, editing or lighting effects) and cultural codes, such as body language, dress or use of colour.

Semiotics appealed greatly to many academics, seeming to offer a scientific framework for analysing the film text, and thereby validating the subject. It offered a system which had its own terminology and was suitably arcane as to require study in order to put it into practice – the mark of a genuine academic subject. Film theorist J. Dudley Andrew observed that the work of textual analysis in applying semiotics had become the identification and analysis of codes: '[the theorist] will explicate it, paying attention to its level of specificity, to its degree of generality, and to its interaction with other codes' (Andrew, 1976, p231). The semiotic approach was founded on a fundamental argument that any representation is a construction, not purely a reflection of reality. The film-maker has made choices in the act of signifying, using a range of filmic elements in order to create meaning. Ultimately, in terms of textual analysis, this approach rendered all aspects of the visual and sound elements of film as meaningful, and therefore worthy of consideration.

Where are we now?

The semiotic approach to analysis was to have a profound impact upon film studies, primarily in furnishing a systematic method for exploring the codes and conventions of the film text. Nevertheless, the theory is constructed around a fundamental problem with the proposition that cinema is a form of language. Semiotics failed to take account of other key dimensions of cinema, such as technology, industrial context and audience response. As a theory it has informed many subsequent developments within the thinking about film, specifically ideological and psychoanalytic approaches to the film text.

Contemporary thinking around the approach to film analysis embraces a range of different approaches, with no one theory or approach claiming to be *the* future of the subject. This is to be expected of a mature subject, which no longer needs (we hope) to establish its academic credibility. The history of theoretical debates around the essence of film has set the agenda regarding the critical response to the film. As film has matured, it has prompted a series of significant interventions seeking to define the essential nature of cinema, which in turn have influenced approaches to analyses of the film text. It is important to recognize how the theoretical developments have taken place within a wider cultural context in responding to changes in film technology, as with the introduction of sound, or responding to greater political contexts, as with the radical agenda of the Russian formalists. Perhaps it could be argued that the theory of each era is a response to developments in film style, which can be fully understood by the social and cultural context.

The contemporary approach to film analysis does not discard previous theory, but acknowledges their shortcomings. Nowell-Smith writes that the way in which films work cannot be described in terms of frameworks of signification: 'films . . . work in less describable ways. They work as painting or music do, partly through meaning but partly in other ways' (Nowell-Smith, 2000, p16). For him, the application of a rational schema such as semiotics in order to interrogate film meaning does not do the text justice; it is time to go back to theories of the aesthetic, which were jettisoned in the 1970s.

Summary

- The analysis of film style is central to the discipline of film studies.
- The analysis of film style is centred on the interaction of the web of elements of film 'language'; no one element should be considered in isolation.
- The consideration of a film's formal techniques should take the wider context of production and exhibition into consideration.
- Two opposed approaches – formalist and realist – characterized early film theory concerning the style and purpose of film.
- Semiotics provided a rational schema for approaching analysis of the film text, although tending to be associated with debates around deciphering the ideological aspects of film.
- Film studies has witnessed a resurgence of interest in aesthetics.
- Thinking about these issues and theories will help you to develop an awareness of different critical approaches, along with a sensitivity to different aspects of the film text.

References and further reading

Andrew, J. D. (1976) *The Major Film Theories*, Oxford University Press, Oxford

Balazs, B. (1952) *Theory of the Film*, Dennis Dobson, London

Bazin, A. (1967) *What is Cinema?*, University of California Press, Berkeley, CA

Gibbs, J. and Pye, D. (2005) *Style and Meaning*, Manchester University Press, Manchester

Nowell-Smith, G. (2000) 'How films mean, or from aesthetics to semiotics and half-way back again', in C. Gledhill and L. Williams (eds) *Reinventing Film Studies*, Arnold, London, pp8–17

Perkins, V. F. (1993) *Film as Art: Understanding and Judging the Movies*, Da Capo Press, New York, NY

Pudovkin, V. (1958) *Film Technique and Film Acting*, Mayflower Memorial Edition, Vision, London

The classic text for many years which is still included on most university reading lists is David Bordwell and Kristin Thompson's *Film Art: An Introduction* (ninth edition, McGraw-Hill, 2010). It provides an exceptionally thorough introduction to film analysis.

Another very accessible textbook is Timothy Corrigan and Patricia White's *The Film Experience: An Introduction* (Palgrave Macmillan, 2009).

7

Film Studies and Narrative Theories

In this chapter we will consider:

- the development of narratology in the field of film studies;
- the definition of types of narrative conventions;
- the relationship between the audience and narrative;
- the possibility of new types of storytelling in film.

The universality of storytelling

Film is a narrative medium; it doesn't merely reflect the world back to us but organizes events into a story. Even documentaries are structured into a story for the audience to engage with. Narrative is a way of constructing the 'world' – or diegesis – of a film, and it is governed by a series of conventions which, in turn, create expectations for the audience. The aim of mainstream film narrative, particularly that of Hollywood cinema, is to make these conventions appear natural so that the audience forgets it is a construction. Even the most fantastical films, those that deal with science fiction or fantasy worlds, are made to appear believable for the duration of the film. It is easy to accept a narrative structure as natural because it is so familiar and every day. We use narrative to organize the way in which we tell experiences to friends – for example, to recount what happened on a night out. In recounting an event, a variety of options present themselves: to tell it chronologically or to start at the end of the night and work backwards; how to introduce the different people – or characters – involved; how much information to reveal and at which point of the story, and so on. All of these decisions are made almost subconsciously, but all will have an effect on the entertainment or shock value of the story, how the listener reacts to particular events and how they judge the different participants.

In film studies, the study of narrative, known as narratology, is concerned with the structural similarities and function of narratives across film. In other words, it examines how films tell stories and why they take the form they do. In this way narratology is often more concerned with the structural aspects of film than with the detailed subject matter. This emphasis led to accusations that it was too general as an approach, that it didn't take into account the specifics of film style in the way that auteur theory – where the emphasis was on detailed textual analysis of the *mise en scène* – did.

Film form and storytelling

The history of the development of film form has tended to be seen as a series of inevitable technological advancements developed by the need for greater realism and more immersive storytelling, the two being seen as inextricably linked. Key among these developments was continuity editing, with its emphasis on cause and effect, and the ability to construct a logical time and place. In addition, the close-up provided the opportunity to study faces, character and emotions, which in turn provoked empathy in the audience. The introduction of sound recording during the late 1920s meant that complex plots and relationships could now be transmitted quickly and more literally than through the inter-titles and symbolism of silent cinema. The development of colour meant that the world on screen was more recognizably like the real world than when it was represented in black and white (the recent use of 3D technology could also be added to the list). In this account, the technological and formal history of cinema is explained by the desire for a more intricate storytelling mode and verisimilitude; to make film on a flat screen seem real and three-dimensional for the audience. Here, narrative is more important than spectacle, with developments in film style led by the desire to tell stories. There are, though, counter-voices to this argument, notably Tom Gunning (1990), whose history of early cinema describes it as a 'cinema of attractions' where audience pleasure did not rely solely on the identification with character or the following of a plot. The dominance of narrative cinema globally, backed up by the institutional dominance of Hollywood, has now left little room for non-narrative cinema;

but in the 1920s, experiments in film form – for example, in surrealist film movements – were evident.

Another way of analysing this type of narrative film-making was through an approach termed 'poetics', which was developed in *The Classical Hollywood Cinema* (1985) by Bordwell, Thompson and Staiger. Rather than an ideological account of mainstream film-making, this set out to identify the formal norms of film production from a particular institution at a particular time – in this case, Hollywood film production from the beginnings of the studio system up until 1960.

Thompson (1999) defines the key characteristics of contemporary Hollywood storytelling, or classical narrative, as one in which unified narratives are central and function through a series of cause-and-effect relationships. The aim of this type of narrative is to have all the effects in the story motivated by a cause which is either immediately apparent or becomes so in retrospect (the 'dangling cause'). Hollywood films are characterized by the closure of all plots and sub-plots; even when a film is to be followed by a sequel there is none of the ambiguity of an open ending associated with non-Hollywood cinema; instead, it aims to guide the audience to an expectation about the next film in the series. The forward progression towards an inevitable ending is motivated throughout, reinforcing the verisimilitude of the narrative; it couldn't happen any other way. Motivation is usually based on character traits (set up very quickly at the beginning of the film) which rely on a character behaving consistently throughout the story; any deviation from established traits must, in turn, be motivated to avoid inexplicable actions or plot 'holes'. The character traits and motivations propel the protagonist towards the end to the fulfilment of a series of goals. Bordwell (2006) defines a series of norms, or principles, of storytelling which are crucial to most Hollywood films. These include goal orientation and the double plotline, both of which link to the primary characters, such as the protagonist and antagonist. The narrative progression is driven by their desire to attain goals, overcoming a range of obstacles in their way. For the protagonist, these goals emerge from at least two plotlines, one of which will include romantic love. Hollywood film can also be broken into a discrete part structure, with each part revolving around the success or failure of the characters to achieve their goals; Bordwell argues that these parts last approximately 25 to 35 minutes and can be found across all Hollywood storytelling. Borwell's identification of the discrete part structure challenges the conventional analysis of Hollywood films conforming to a three-act structure: here it is often told in four parts. In this, Bordwell's analysis differs from the analysis provided by many screenwriters in a range of instructional books on the practice of scriptwriting.

Narrative and scriptwriting

A major body of work on narrative in film studies has been produced outside of academia by scriptwriters who have published books aiming to teach people how to write a Hollywood screenplay. In order to do this, writers such as Syd Field and Robert McKee have analysed how a Hollywood film is constructed, and in doing so have argued that successful Hollywood films are remarkably similar in structure, following a three-act structure which contains a set-up, development and resolution. This work, aimed at an audience of practitioners, has resulted in many of the ideas of structuralism being recognized by a much wider non-academic audience. The work of screenplay writers also has a specific place in the development of doing film studies as it exists in between film theory and film practice (see Chapter 9 for further analysis of the role of creative practice in film studies). In a related development, film studies has begun to acknowledge the status of screenplays as an important but undervalued aspect of cinema which is worthy of analysis, with screenplays by, among others, Michel Gondry and Charlie Kaufmann now studied.

In his more recent work, David Bordwell (2006, 2011a, 2011b) has analysed Hollywood films which don't seem to conform to the classical narrative model. Films such as *Inception* (2010) and *Source Code* (2011) are described as 'intriguing wrinkles' in the recent history of American studio storytelling. By this Bordwell means that when films innovate in their storytelling practices, they do so through careful reference to established conventions and ensure that any new narrative strategies are made clear to the audience through repetition. Bordwell demonstrates these developments through an analysis of *Source Code*, a sci-fi thriller in which the hero is repeatedly sent back in time for a period of 15 minutes to try to defuse a bomb and save the passengers on a train. While the film does not initially seem to conform to classical narrative structure, Bordwell argues that it still uses several recognizable strategies, such as the discrete part structure (including epilogue), double plotline and identification with a hero. As with any thriller, it utilizes tactics to construct suspense, such as restricted narration (the audience only know as much as the hero) and the way in which the hero is set a series of goals which must be completed against the clock. The innovation of *Source Code* and films like it is the use of what Bordwell defines as a 'forking path' or 'multiple draft' narrative. This narrative structure relies on repetition and is characterized by the replaying of key scenes with variations; but it always remains within the conventions of classical narrative structure. Despite superficially appearing to be a new kind of narrative, Bordwell argues that there hasn't been any fundamental change in the nature of Hollywood storytelling since the 1930s. This view of Hollywood narrative as remaining unchanged since the classical phase has been strongly countered by other film theorists. In *Puzzle Films* (2009), a collection of essays analysing films such as *Fight Club* (1999), *Memento* (2000), *The Butterfly Effect* (2004) and *Lost Highway* (1997),Warren Buckland argues that these films, in their use of multiple draft plotting, do represent a new form of narrative structure in Hollywood. The complexity of the narratives of 'puzzle' or 'mind game' films cannot be reduced to conform to the traditional analysis of narrative norms in Hollywood. Instead, in Buckland's analysis, they are distinct in that they 'break the boundaries of the classical, unified mimetic plot. The puzzle film is made up of non classical characters who perform non classical actions and events' (Buckland, 2009, p5). Another challenge to Bordwell and Thompson's work came from those who rejected the poetic approach itself, arguing that the refusal to interpret film led to a soulless analysis which doesn't deal with the subtleties of meaning and expression in individual films. Within the context of doing film, Bordwell and Thompson's methodology can be understood as an attempt to develop an approach which is more accessible and relevant than film theory, but more academically rigorous than the cinephilia of reviewers and film societies.

Structuralism and the development of narrative theory

The introduction of narrative analysis into film studies as a discipline during the 1960s was part of the reaction against the dominance of auteur theory (see Chapter 4 for a discussion of genre theory in relation to auteur theory). In the film departments of British universities, this was part of a wider theoretical movement known as structuralism. Structuralism, which was based on the study of linguistics and semiotics, aimed to provide an almost scientific framework for the analysis of film. While auteur theory relied on the romantic ideal of the great artist and the value judgements of particular critics, structuralism was hailed as an objective method of uncovering how films worked, removed from an interpretive analysis of style and themes which was purely subjective. The result of this was to produce a body of research which demonstrated the complex nature of popular film narrative, a style which had often been dismissed as simplistic. The danger of this approach was that it would lose sight of the film itself, along with any discussion of the range of audience pleasures available. Structuralism was also used to bolster film studies' claim to be an academic subject with its own methodology, and its approach to narrative structures provided a way of discussing popular culture (film) in a serious academic way. This emphasis on a structural approach ultimately created a split between different areas of film studies, with film theory – as the structuralist approaches became known – associated with university departments, and auteur theory and textual analysis linked to schools, sixth form colleges and film societies.

Narrative theory in film studies treats film as primarily a storytelling medium and looks at how it overlaps with other storytelling forms such as literature, myths and folk tales. Much of the key work in this area is influenced by work in the fields of literary theory, anthropology and sociology. Film theorists have analysed similarities across films to determine whether a particular style of storytelling is typical of a time and place, and, if so, why this particular style has developed.

Components of storytelling: Narrative and narration

The terms narrative and narration are often used interchangeably when talking about film, but have specific meanings which are central to the way in which narrative has been analysed in film, marking it as different than the way in which stories are told in other forms. Narrative in film refers to the elements which constitute the story, plot and characters; narration is the way in which those elements are communicated to the spectator. The latter includes the organization or structure of the story, whether it is told sequentially or in flashback, etc. It also refers to the aesthetic or micro-elements of *mise en scène*, editing, framing and sound which are the form through which the narrative is transmitted. The function of narration in film is not the objective recounting of a story, but the construction of a viewpoint through which the film is received in order to create engagement with the audience and to convince the audience of the truthfulness of what they see. In mainstream cinema, the construction of this viewpoint is often achieved through the alignment with characters who reinforce the messages and values – or ideology – of the film. For example, in *Winter's Bone* (2010), the narrative focuses on a young woman, Ree, who lives in an isolated community in the Ozark Mountains, and it follows her quest to keep her family together, to save her house and to find out what happened to her father. The narration is chronological and constructed to force the audience to align with Ree and to support her desire to achieve her goals. This is done through a variety of techniques; but one important one is the use of restricted – rather than omniscient – narration. In restricted narration the audience is given information at the same time as the central character. Omniscient narration places the audience in a privileged position, knowing more than the characters.

The term narrative structure is used to refer to the way in which film's narrative is organized into a specific form such as a beginning, middle and end, and is central to the work of structural theorists. Approaches to film narrative have been greatly influenced by the work of Vladimir Propp and Tzvetan Todorov, whose work focused on the analysis of literary narratives. The subsequent application of this work to film texts revealed both similarities and differences across the forms. In both cases, the finding that myths and folk tales were structured around repetitions was interpreted by those applying the model to film as ideological. These models were reassuring and hierarchical, emphasizing, particularly in the work of Propp, the norms of hierarchical societal relationships and the drive towards marriage and family as a resolution in stories. The criticisms of these approaches have focused on the lack of textual specificity in the analysis, which emphasizes the similarity rather than differences between films and may also ignore the changing cultural context.

In 'The poetics of prose', Todorov (1977) develops a theory of narrative drawing on the work of the Russian literary formalists, and applied it to the novella form. The analysis is specific to literature, with the grammar of storytelling defined in relation to the differences between adjectives and verbs. Todorov provides a summary of the 'minimal complete plot' which has become a foundation of film narrative analysis:

> An 'ideal' narrative begins with a stable situation, which is disturbed by some power or force. There results a state of disequilibrium; by the action of a force directed in the opposite direction, the equilibrium is re-established; the second equilibrium is similar to the first, but the two are never identical. (Todorov, 1977, p213)

The influence of Propp's analysis of characters demonstrates the concerns that some critics had that structuralism had gone too far, that it was in danger of obliterating the film itself. In *Morphology of the Folk Tale*, Propp (1968) developed an analysis of folk tales which demonstrated that particular characters – the prince, the princess, king, queen, donor, and so on – appeared repeatedly across folk tales from different periods and cultures. This repetition suggested that the characters weren't important for their individual characteristics and personalities, but for their function in the plot. The princess's function was to be rescued; the prince to be the rescuer; the donor or helper was there to provide help to the hero, and so on. In this analysis the detail of particular characters in particular films, their relationship with each other and to their time and place, has little importance. A hero from a film during the 1930s is essentially the same as one from today: their appearance, attitudes and gender may have changed but their function remains the same.

For proponents of this formalist approach to film narrative analysis, this allowed connections to be made across film history, to identify the similarities in films rather than the differences. A popular example used to illustrate this has been the comparison of *The Searchers* (1956) and *Taxi Driver* (1976). Both films have a central hero who is an outsider who is driven by pessimism about the future of their society. Both heroes rescue a princess who may not have wanted to be rescued. While the similarities in the structure of the two films is clear, critics of such an approach might question how useful such a recognition is, whether it reveals anything new about the meanings of the film, the different periods in which they were produced, or the audience's response to them. It may demonstrate the similarities in film storytelling style across the decades; but does it illuminate the differences in the period which produced them? In what can be considered a counterargument to the accusations of empty analysis, structural theorists also developed their approach to look at the wider function of narratives, arguing that popular film narrative was an ideological form.

Narrative theory and ideology

In narrative theory, the construction of meaning in a film is produced by structural relationships, specifically oppositional categories which carry particular connotations. This approach was based on the structural analysis of myths developed by the anthropologist Claude Lévi-Strauss, who argued that myths are organized around a series of binary oppositions. These are mutually exclusive categories which are fundamental to our understanding of the world: male not female, land not sea, good not bad, etc. In myths (and therefore, it was assumed, also in popular films), the ideological message could be understood by tracing the narrative development and resolution. The meaning was usually carried in the role of the protagonist; therefore, by tracing which side of the opposition the protagonist ended up on at the film's resolution, the ideology of the film was evident.

This approach was more successful with some films and genres than others; much influential work was produced on the western which seemed to lend itself to the analysis of binary oppositions and the role of the hero. In his influential analysis of the western genre, *Six Guns and Society* (1975), Will Wright argues that westerns are structured around the binary oppositions of civilization and wilderness, with the hero mediating between the two before aligning with the side of civilization, represented by white homesteaders and Christianity, rather than the wilderness of pagan Native Americans.

Criticisms of this approach suggested that it was reductionist and too narrow in its ideological reading. David Bordwell (2011a) takes issue with the argument that film is inherently ideological because it would mean that 'to experience a classic western is to buy at least partly into its racist assumptions'. But it has been extremely influential as an analytical tool and has been used to examine the construction of meaning in films beyond the western. In his structural analysis of the rom com/caper film *Desperately Seeking Susan* (1987), Graeme Turner (1999) shows how the central character of Susan, a repressed suburban housewife, rejects the values of mainstream society in 'an unusually strong attack on suburban marriage'. Here the western's oppositions of the wilderness and civilization are transposed to New York and their meanings subverted, and the structural analysis works to provide convincing evidence for a feminist reading of the film.

The importance of analysing film form and narrative theory for structural theorists such as Peter Wollen (1972) and Colin McCabe (1974) was based on the understanding that form was ideological; there was a direct link between the way in which a story was told and its ideology. In this analysis, structure is clearly dominant over the content; there is no possibility of a narrative film containing a radical ideology: it will always reinforce the status quo. This reading of mainstream film meant that a film which seemed to have a liberal storyline, perhaps around issues of gender equality or civil rights, is only superficially progressive because the narrative form functions to reinforce rather than subvert existing structures in society. Mainstream films which deal with political or social issues in order to highlight injustices in society – for example, *Mississippi Burning* (1988), *Erin Brockovich* (2000), *Crash* (2004), *Michael Clayton* (2007), *Ides of March* (2011) – still rely on a conventional structure and style, often using the thriller genre where the plot is driven by the discovery of the 'truth' by a lone hero, who then resolves the problems revealed. This mainstream narrative form does not allow for a political analysis of society or a questioning of the fundamental beliefs of individualism and free enterprise. The reliance on a cause-and-effect narrative structure, the need for resolution and the specific role of the hero means that it isn't possible.

This analysis of Hollywood film was defined as the 'classic realist text'. The phrase has the specific meaning of an ideologically conservative cinema which positions the audience to accept a single message. McCabe (1974) defined the classic realist text in film as presenting the world in an unproblematic way to the viewer through the narration. This dominant film style relies on a series of characteristics which create a range of effects for the audience. These effects include provoking an emotional response through identification with characters, while the repeated patterns of the classic narrative form reassure the audience that any film they see won't be very different from any other. The classic narrative structure in its emphasis on equilibrium and repetition resolves all the problems, and therefore the passive spectator accepts this as truthful.

In order to counter this passive state and acceptance of the ideology transmitted by the film, Wollen (1972) argued for a new kind of film practice, a counter-cinema which would subvert the conventions of Hollywood cinema and, in turn, force the audience to become more active.

Narrative theory in practice: Counter-cinema

The attack on Hollywood cinema as an ideological practice argued that cinema shapes rather than reflects the desires of the audience. It is a form of propaganda which reinforces bourgeois values through a series of repeated images and ideas. These include the concept of the romantic ideal and domestic bliss, the pleasures of poverty, the role of women and a belief in the ability of an individual to change the world. Hollywood film makes what is constructed appear natural through its use of a particular film style, which hides its status as film-making; in effect, it appears like a window on the world. In order to disrupt these ideological messages, it was argued that it wasn't enough to change the subject matter; the very form of film would have to be subverted. This would force the audience to look at film in a new way and not just accept its messages passively. To challenge this there should be a counter-cinema, a form of theory in practice. Developed by Peter Wollen (1972) through an analysis of the films by the French director Jean-Luc Godard, the concept of counter-cinema was typical of theoretical approaches during the late 1960s and 1970s, which drew on Marxist theory and were interested in the way film could be part of a revolutionary process. In defining counter-cinema (or oppositional cinema), Wollen conceived of a series of binary oppositions between the classic realist film and a new revolutionary cinema. Narrative would no longer be based on cause-and-effect, leading to an inevitable conclusion, but would be elliptical and fragmented without relying on an individual hero for the audience to align with. Instead of trying to hide the film construction through invisible editing, the construction of the film would be foregrounded through jump cuts and even scratching marks on the film stock itself. Overall, the smooth, harmonious world of the film was to be disrupted to prevent the audience losing themselves in a fantasy world. Examples of counter-cinema are found in Third Cinema, avant-garde and experimental film, proving to be a demanding watch for the audience due to its explicit aim of non-pleasure. It was, though, in the context of feminist film theory and practice that the concept of counter-cinema was particularly influential, where it became part of the discussion about gender and narrative.

Narrative theory and feminist approaches

The key texts in the feminist analysis of classic narrative were by the British film theorists Laura Mulvey and Claire Johnstone, and their work continues to influence current debates about film and gender. According to Mulvey, in her seminal essay 'Visual pleasure and narrative cinema' (1975), the pleasure of watching Hollywood film was a heterosexual, erotic pleasure with images of women displayed – or objectified – for the gratification of the male spectator, and this was a result of the specific narrative form and visual style used by Hollywood. Mulvey argued that pleasure for the audience in watching a film comes from a form of spying on others (on the screen) without being seen. This is an example of voyeurism, which is particularly associated with *looking* to gain sexual pleasure. The cinema conditions are ideal for this: the dark auditorium where the audience is separated from each other; the screen which creates the illusion of looking into a private world which seems real (the suspension of disbelief). Classic narrative film also offers idealized characters, heroes to identify with, whose world we share. We are encouraged to recognize ourselves in these ideal figures that are actually better looking, stronger, more intelligent and more successful than we are. This identification is therefore a form of narcissism (or vanity) because the hero is superior to us. Through identification, which is a central characteristic of narrative film, it is the male hero who transmits the look of the male cinema spectator. It is a privileged position as the male spectator sees the female character through the eyes of the hero – sharing the power of the hero (for further discussion of feminist film theory, see Chapters 5 and 8).

This structure of looking and identification in the cinema affects the form of the narrative – women looked at as erotic objects slow down the story; women become static while the male is active, moving the story forward. It is this model which has been defined as the 'male gaze'; the male spectator simultaneously identifies with the hero and looks at the female for erotic pleasure. In feminist film theory of this period, the solution to this inherently sexist film form was to construct a new kind of cinema, one which would challenge the existing structure and style. Examples of this new kind of film-making included *Riddle of the Sphinx*, a short film co-directed by Laura Mulvey and Peter Wollen, which is also indicative of the integration of theory and practice of the period. The work of the British film-maker Sally Potter is also influenced by counter-cinema in both her early experimental films such as *Thriller* and later crossover films, including *Orlando*, *Tango* and *Yes*.

Summary

- Narratology provided an academic, pseudo-scientific approach to the study of film form.
- Narratology is more concerned with similarities between films rather than differences.
- Dominant narrative forms have been characterized as ideological.
- The field of narrative analysis has encouraged the integration of theory and practice.

References and further reading

Bordwell, D. (2006) *The Way Hollywood Tells It*, University of California Press, Berkeley, CA

Bordwell, D. (2011a) 'Academics versus critics', *Film Comment*, http://www.filmlinc.com/film-comment/article/never-the-twain-shall-meet

Bordwell, D. (2011b) 'Forking tracks: *Source Code*', 3 May, Observations on Film Art, http://www.davidbordwell.net/blog/2011/05/03/forking-tracks-source-code/, accessed 26 April 2012

Bordwell, D., Thompson, K. and Staiger, J. (1985) *The Classical Hollywood Cinema*, Routledge, London

Buckland, W. (2009) 'Introduction: Puzzle plots', in W. Buckland (ed) *Puzzle Films: Complex Storytelling in Contemporary Film*, Wiley-Blackwell, Oxford

Dix, A. (2008) *Beginning Film Studies*, Manchester University Press, Manchester, pp105–108

Field, S. (1979) *Screenplay*, Bantam, New York, NY

Gunning, T. (1990) 'The cinema of attractions: Early film, its spectator and the avant-garde', in T. Elsaesser (ed) *Early Cinema: Space, Frame, Narrative*, British Film Institute, London

McCabe, C. (1974) 'From realism and the cinema: Notes on some Brechtian theses', in A. Easthope (ed, 1993) *Contemporary Film Theory*, Longman, New York, NY, pp53–67

McKee, R. (1997) *Story: Substance, Structure, Style and the Principles of Screenwriting*, Regan Books, New York, NY

Mulvey, L. (1975) 'Visual pleasure and narrative cinema', *Screen*, vol 16, no 3, pp6–18

Propp, V. (1968) *Morphology of the Folk Tale*, University of Texas Press, Austin, TX

Thompson, K. (1999) *Storytelling in the New Hollywood: Understanding Classical Narrative Technique*, Harvard University Press, Cambridge, MA

Todorov, T. (1977) 'The poetics of prose', in D. Hale (ed, 2006) *The Novel: An Anthology of Criticism*, Blackwell, Oxford, pp205–219

Turner, G. (1999) *Film as Social Practice*, third edition, Routledge, London

Wollen, P. (1972) 'Conclusion', in P. Wollen (ed) *Signs and Meaning in the Cinema*, Secker and Warburg, London, pp155–174

Wollen, P. (1985) 'Vent d'Est', in B. Nicholls (ed) *Movies and Methods, Volume 2*, University of California, Berkeley, CA

Wright, W. (1975) *Six Guns and Society*, University of California Press, Berkeley, CA

David Bordwell's website (http://www.davidbordwell.net/) is a very useful and entertaining resource for the study of narrative. It contains extracts from his published works, as well as a series of blogs and discussions on a diverse range of films and narrative approaches.

Thomas Elsaesser's 'The mind game film' in W. Buckland (ed.) *Puzzle Films: Complex Storytelling in Contemporary Film* (Wiley-Blackwell, 2009) defines the characteristics of the mind game film, considers the reasons for its emergence and popularity, and argues that it constitutes a different type of narrative form than classical Hollywood film.

Recent developments in narratology have considered the influence of video games on narrative films. In 'S/Z, the "readerly" film, and video game logic (*The Fifth Element*)' Warren Buckland and Thomas Elsaesser (*Studying Contemporary American Film: A Guide to Movie Analysis*, Arnold, 2002) define the concept of the digital narrative and debate the role of interactivity in film.

8

Spectatorship and Audience Studies

In this chapter we will consider:

- why the concept of the spectator is important in film studies;
- how film studies moved from referring to the spectator to discussing the audience;
- what is meant by the 'imaginary' spectator;
- how film studies has been influenced by other disciplines in analysing the relationship between audience and film.

There are a variety of different ways of looking at the audience in film studies. These include the relationship between the individual spectator and the film, the different ways of experiencing the film in the wider culture (such as marketing, celebrity magazines, merchandise, etc.), as well as the intersection between the audience and the film industry. Discussion of the audience is now acknowledged as an important, even vital, aspect of film studies; but this hasn't always been the case. In the history of film studies as a subject, the spectator was initially ignored completely. The development of spectatorship theory and audience studies was then characterized by the conception of the spectator as a single homogeneous entity, followed finally by a recognition of the way in which audiences are made up of a variety of different backgrounds and experiences that can lead to a range of different interpretations of specific films. This shift in the way that film studies talks about the audience has been greatly influenced, first, by psychoanalysis and, more recently, by approaches developed in cultural and media studies (such as reception studies). It is this shift in influences which has led to the changes in terminology in discussing the audience. The psychoanalytic approach makes reference to a single spectator who is constructed by the film itself (or text in this context). Later theories acknowledge the existence of multiple audiences. Therefore, to use the term spectator or audience in film studies is to imply differing approaches and interpretations.

How and where is meaning created in film?

Early approaches to the study of film, before the advent of film theory or the intersection with related academic disciplines, tended to ignore the audience. This was due to the emphasis on authorship as the dominant approach to explaining film (see Chapters 2 and 3 for more discussion of auteur theory). In auteur theory, it was understood that meaning was placed in the film by the author (the director) where it remained fixed, understood by all members of the audience in exactly the same way. In this model of how meaning is created in film, the film would have the same meaning whether it was projected in an empty room and no one ever watched it or if it was screened to a global audience repeatedly for over 50 years. This analysis of the creation of meaning was typical of traditional approaches to discussing high art where the artist was seen as separate from society and was the sole creator of meaning in their work.

One of the criticisms of auteur theory was that it ignored the audience, which (given that cinema is a social experience) was to ignore a major aspect of what makes film different from other art forms. This 'problem' of a film studies dominated by auteur theory was addressed by two differing approaches. Genre theory acknowledged the existence and importance of the audience by studying popular films which were enjoyed by a mass audience. Its key contribution to audience studies was the idea that audience members understand genre films in the context of all the other films they've seen belonging to that genre, and that audience taste may, in part, be responsible for the type of films produced (see Chapter 4 for a detailed discussion of the development of genre theory in film studies). The influence of screen theory in university film departments meant that its development of spectatorship theory, heavily influenced by psychoanalysis, became the dominant approach to thinking about the relationship between the film and the spectator. These ideas were driven by the question of how meaning is created in film-making and film-viewing, and what this says about the attraction of watching films. In the reliance on a psychoanalytic explanation for how film is experienced, the answers to these questions involved the concepts of the unconscious mind and desire.

Psychoanalysis and cinema

Film studies began to draw on psychoanalysis during the 1970s. In some ways it is surprising that it was not taken up earlier given that cinema and psychoanalysis were developed at the same time (Sigmund Freud's *Interpretation of Dreams* was published in 1897, while the first projected films are usually dated to around the same year), and literary theory had applied Freudian readings of novels since the 1930s and 1940s. The move towards psychoanalysis was provoked by dissatisfaction with structuralism and its attempt to provide a total theory of film. Psychoanalysis was part of a post-structuralist movement which engaged with the idea that the spectator created meaning in a text rather than the text simply creating the spectator response, so that the spectator becomes more active in the construction of meaning. In this context, theorists discussed the way in which the spectator 'affected' the text as well as how the text 'affected' the spectator. This was the first shift towards a recognition that the meaning does not just reside in the film but is created through a meeting between the film and the spectator. Chapter 5 discusses the development and influence of screen theory with reference to the key elements of psychoanalytic film theory; in this section we will consider how effective these approaches have been in explaining the relationship between the spectator and the film with specific reference to the study of stars.

The relevance of psychoanalysis to film studies is often explained through the similarity between films and dreams. Therefore, it was argued, the focus in psychoanalysis on dreams and the world of the unconscious mind to explain human behaviour could be transferred to films. In doing this, film theory also took on board the emphasis on sexuality and desire central to psychoanalysis. For Freud, the location of desire is the gap between the real and the imaginary, the gap between the world as it is and as we would desire it to be. This idea seemed to be fairly easily applicable to the status of film as a form; film mirrors the world around us so that it will appear real, to the point that the spectator is convinced of its reality; but, simultaneously, film is imaginary. For several theorists it was the way in which film collapsed the boundaries between the real and the unreal which made it so attractive; film existed in the gap between the real and the imaginary and was therefore the location of desire. John Ellis, a film theorist influenced by psychoanalysis, explains the attraction of film for the spectator in a way which demonstrates it to be a dynamic one where the spectator is constantly moving between the real and the imaginary. Ellis argues that the fascination of film is so strong for the spectator that they desire to enter the film 'to disrupt even the minimal boundaries which divide the imaginary and the real in cinema' (1982, p81). This idea of the spectator crossing the boundary between the imaginary and the real in cinema is the basis for the Woody Allen film *The Purple Rose of Cairo* (1985). Set in Depression-era America of the 1930s, it is about a woman who finds solace and escapism at the cinema: her desire to escape her life is so great that it creates a rupture between her world and the world of the film, with screen characters entering the real world and vice versa.

The specific power which film exerts over the spectator has also been explained by its use of a particular type of narrative and editing techniques. Defined as suture – or stitching – this refers to the way in which the spectator interprets a film. The theory of suture was influenced by Lacanian psycho-analysis and developed by the influential post-structuralist film theorist Ste-phen Heath and the social scientist Daniel Dayan. Suture was a way of explaining the ideological power of film, arguing that it positions the specta-tor to receive a single message but to hide the way in which this is done. Due to the nature of continuity editing in classic Hollywood cinema, the meaning of a shot only becomes clear when we see the following shot. This creates an on-going narrative drive where the spectator is constantly creating the mean-ing between the present shot and the next one; the spectator is 'suturing' together the shots in order to be able to understand the narrative. This is done almost unconsciously and naturally so that the spectator is unaware of the means of construction of a film. This process creates a form of desire – a desire to constantly see the next shot as well as a desire to reach a resolution, to find out the overall meaning of the narrative. In this way, the spectator is caught in a position of wanting the film to continue, to see the next shot, but also wanting the film to end. It is these contradictory impulses which create desire and therefore the fascination with film. The theory of suture provides the foundation for seeing the spectator as part of meaning construction; but the conclusion of suture theorists was that this was part of a process which resulted in a mass unthinking audience who all receive the same message. This ideological interpretation of the relationship between spectator and text was criticized for ignoring the influence of different spectators' experiences as well as the diversity of films experienced.

Psychoanalytic film theory remains an influential aspect of film studies, particularly in the context of feminist film theory, but has been criticized from various positions. The appropriateness of the analogy of dreams and film has been questioned; films have a soundtrack while dreams do not, and the extent to which films are the product of the unconscious mind is also debatable. The use of psychoanalysis also limits the function and meaning of film – films become the bearer of fantasies for the spectator rather than anything else. Similarly, this approach has been criticized for being a reductive one, only allowing one explanation for the relationship between film and the spectator. In this case it is apparently explained through the spectator seeing film through the filter of the unconscious, which doesn't allow any room for other 'filters' such as personal experience, conditions of viewing, time and place, etc. A further criticism is that it ignores the way in which spectators understand film through social influences and conscious effort as much as through the unconscious. In arguing that the spectator was positioned by the text, through the apparatus of cinema, psychoanalytic film theory made the films and the spectator homogeneous – as if there was only one film and one spectator. Some of the counterarguments to this conception of the spectator came from theorists who were also influenced by psychoanalysis but saw some of the limitations in how it had been applied to films and spectators so far. Dudley Andrew (1984), a critic of psychoanalytic theory, placed the specific nature of the film itself in the centre of his explanation of the relationship between the spectator and the film. In this analysis, the power of the film does come from its effect on the psyche, but only within the context of a specific cinematic context; different types of films will have different effects on the spectator.

While psychoanalytic approaches privileged the unconscious as the way of explaining the film's effects on the spectator, there have also been attempts to widen out this focus to explain the visceral, physiological effect which watching films can also have. The development of an approach which examined the 'affective' dimension of film developed out of a need to discuss the sensuous and tactile responses to film in a serious way. References to film provoking a physiological response have usually been found in the context of popular culture being discussed like a drug, used pejoratively to provide evidence that film was a feeling rather than thinking medium. This is also evident in references to blockbusters providing a 'roller-coaster ride' for the spectator, a term which is used to signify superficiality rather than a serious, thoughtful film. The concept of affect recognizes the powerful response elicited by film, but doesn't consider it in terms of a value judgement – rather, it is important to understand how and why film can provoke such a response: '[film] is a vivid medium, and it is important to talk about how it arouses corporeal reactions of desire and fear, pleasure and disgust, fascination and shame' (Shaviro, 1993).Work in this area has been particularly concerned with how audiences view violence and why violence on screen can be pleasurable to watch. This affective approach is a new way to discuss violent films, in response to the media studies approach of effects theory which examines the idea that watching violent films can lead to individuals acting violently.

Affect theory is one way of challenging psychoanalysis's dominance in discussing spectatorship, arguing that film is not a medium which can purely be explained by reference to desire and the unconscious. Further arguments have pointed out the need to recognize the variety of pleasures which film – as part of popular culture – also provides. These include the pleasures of recognition and familiarity found in classic narrative and genre film-making, film as part of a social event, and the extra-textual pleasures found in reading about films and in following particular stars. This acknowledgement that extra-textual influences are also important led to a division within spectatorship theory in film studies. Influenced by developments in other disciplines, particularly cultural studies, there was recognition in film studies that the meaning of the text was not inherent and fixed; instead there could be multiple meanings created by a range of audience members who bring their own backgrounds and experience to their interpretation. This was a major development in film studies, signalling the recognition that the audience was made up of a variety of different people who could all bring their own meaning to the film. These ideas were particularly influenced by the work of Stuart Hall at the Centre for Cultural Studies and Research. Hall (1980) argued that although there may be a 'preferred meaning' in a text (including film), the audience member was actually able to reject or accept it, to negotiate the meaning or to create an oppositional one. The recognition of this meant that the discussion of the spectator in film studies shifted from being primarily aesthetic, focused on the workings of the film form, to an understanding of the importance of events outside of the film – and the cinema itself.

Audience studies and stars

The different approaches to theorizing the audience in film studies can be illustrated in the specific area of star studies. Although there had been a great deal of writing about stars in terms of celebrity magazine coverage, interviews, gossip and biographies, star studies as an academic approach only emerged during the mid-1970s. The key aim of star studies has been to ask why certain actors become stars and other – perhaps equally attractive and talented – actors don't, what this tells us about the appeal of stars for an audience, and, in turn, what that might suggest about the values of the society which produced the stars. In examining the relationship between stars and the audience, theorists have applied ideological, psychoanalytic and ethnographic approaches, mirroring the wider developments in audience studies as a whole. One of the most influential theorists in developing an analysis of stars is Richard Dyer, whose book *Stars* (1979) was one of the founding texts of the area.

Dyer's approach allows the study of stars to go beyond the belief in certain individuals who are imbued with magical qualities (beauty, talent, etc.) and looks at them in relation to ideological issues such as class, race, gender and sexual orientation. The purpose of this kind of study is to reveal the meanings behind stars which may not be immediately apparent and uses approaches from semiotic analysis to deconstruct the meaning attached to a particular performer. Therefore, a star can be defined as a sign which also connotes further meanings about attractiveness, masculinity, femininity, race, national identity and definitions of normality in a particular society. An ideological analysis of stars suggests that the meanings behind a star can tell us what a society values and what it rejects. In Dyer's most influential example from *Stars* he analyses the persona of Marilyn Monroe to demonstrate how she represents ideas about sexual identity which were current in the US at the time. In this study, the star image only makes sense when it is interpreted within wider social and cultural contexts, areas which are outside of the film itself and which are extra-textual. This construction of stars is not, for Dyer, an innocent activity but an ideological practice which reinforces dominant values in society. Dyer's work on stars is based on the recognition that what takes place on screen is only one of the elements which creates meaning for the audience. It also assumes that film is an ideological medium, which suggests that it is very hard to resist the representations bound up in a star persona: that the audience is, to an extent, at the mercy of the image. Dyer's later work on the way in which audiences interpret images has allowed far more scope for the spectator to resist the meaning of the image and to reinterpret it, an idea which has had particular relevance for gay and queer readings of film.

John Ellis (1982), like Richard Dyer, sees stars as an inter-textual construction in that their meaning is only complete when all the aspects relating to a star both inside and outside of the cinema come together in the spectator's experience. Ellis distinguishes between different components which make up the star persona. There is the dominant (or most meaningful) element, which is the film performance itself, and then the secondary elements. These are the ideas about and coverage of the star which circulate in magazines, on TV and, of course, now in cyberspace. Using a psychoanalytic approach to explain the spectator's desire for a particular star, Ellis states that the audience is compelled to go to the cinema to see the star on film as this is what completes their experience of the star from the incomplete image constructed by the subsidiary texts circulating around them. In a similar way to the earlier ideas about film being the gap between the real and unreal, and therefore the location of desire, Ellis argues that the desire for a star is part of the spectator's need to fulfil what is lacking. In Lacanian psychoanalysis, desire is part of the formation of subjectivity: the constant attempt to restore what is missing or lacking. As this interpretation of desire is fundamentally linked to looking (the concept of voyeurism), viewing film is linked with desire for the star. The spectator identifies with the star, but also enjoys the pleasure of spying on and desiring the star – a form of voyeurism. These simultaneous but contradictory impulses are the very thing which keeps the spectator going back to the cinema in order to satisfy their desires. While the viewer hopes that they will be fulfilled by the star image, in fact, all they are getting is fragments – the close-ups of a star's eyes, legs, mouth – and left unfulfilled they will need to keep returning to the cinema. In this analysis the experience outside of the cinema is an important context for the spectator response, but the psychoanalytic theories of desire and subjectivity are dominant, suggesting that every member of the audience will respond in the same way.

Both ideological and psychoanalytic interpretations of the spectator response to stars assume that the text is the bearer of meaning – in this case, through the star performance. A dramatic break with this approach came through the influence of another cultural studies approach, that of reception studies. Here theorists focused on trying to establish what the actual responses to specific stars by individual audience members were. This approach is used by Jackie Stacey in her influential research into the cinema-going habits of women in the UK during the 1940s and 1950s, which examined the appeal of certain stars. Published as *Stargazing* (1993), Stacey's aim was to integrate aspects of psychoanalytic theories of spectatorship with techniques from ethnographic research in order to construct a more complete understanding of the position of the spectator (in this case, the female spectator). Stacey acknowledges that there are clear differences between the two approaches but also that, within feminist approaches to audience, there are increasing similarities, particularly in determining notions of audience pleasure and identification.

Stacey clarifies the differences between approaches to the audience in film studies and cultural studies through a series of oppositions. In film studies the emphasis is on textual analysis, the passive viewer and the role of the unconscious. In opposition to this, cultural studies uses ethnographic rather than textual methods, and sees the viewer as active and conscious. Overall, she argues, cultural studies has an optimistic view of the relationship between the spectator and the text, while film studies, with its emphasis on the power of the image and ideological readings, is more pessimistic (Stacey, 1993, p24). To gather her research, Stacey placed a letter in two weekly women's magazines asking for readers to volunteer to help with a project on the experience of cinema-going during the 1940s and 1950s. These respondents then filled out a detailed questionnaire about their cinema-going experiences of the time, as well as writing about particular aspects of the wider film culture which they remembered. In analysing the results of this information, Stacey utilized concepts from psychoanalytic approaches to spectatorship, categorizing the different ways in which audience members identified with female stars in the cinema and outside of it. These included the processes of devotion, adoration, worship, aspiration and inspiration. The bringing together of audience research with psychoanalytic concepts meant that Stacey was able to counter influential theories such as the male gaze, demonstrating that the female spectator was active, identifying with characters on screen and even continuing the experience of spectatorship outside of the cinema into the way in which they dressed and acted.

The approach developed in *Stargazing* was to situate spectators in a specific time and place. This introduced the real spectator into film studies in order to counter the concept of the imaginary spectator: an actual person who could identify specific responses and emotions. Stacey's approach did draw criticism on a methodological level. These criticisms highlighted the inadequacy of the reliance on questionnaires as a basis for research. The respondents were self-selecting; the invitation to fill out the questionnaire was framed with reference to Hollywood stars, perhaps skewing the responses and the memories of those interviewed. The fact that the research was only into female spectatorship was also questioned as it seemed to reinforce the assumption that spectatorship is gendered.

The importance of an audience's context in analysing their response to a specific film and the wider film culture has been developed in an approach termed 'cultural geographies', which uses ethnographic research to examine cinema culture in a very specific time and place. Key texts in this emerging area include *The Place of the Audience: Cultural Geographies of Film*

Consumption by Mark Jancovich et al (2003), which traces the history of film exhibition in Nottingham from the early screenings at fairgrounds to the arrival of the multiplex, arguing that the experience of film consumption must be understood in the context of types of exhibition spaces as well as the study of the film itself.

Reception studies and the perverse spectator

Contemporary audience studies have been most influentially shaped by the idea of reception studies. This influence has continued the shift from the focus on the film as the sole creator of meaning to arguing that it is audiences, with all the extra-textual baggage which they carry, who create meaning and interpretation. Janet Staiger (2003), in her influential study of audience responses, titled *Perverse Spectators*, sees 'contextual factors rather than textual material or reader psychologies as most important in illuminating the reading process or interpretation'. For her, the spectator is 'perverse' because they don't conform to the theoretical expectations laid down by spectatorship theory. The ground rules for successful audience research in film studies are, Staiger argues, the acknowledgement of the importance of specific historical and social locations, and the recognition of the complex nature of the film text. Spectators must also not be conceived of as 'empty' when they watch a film, and films do not contain immanent – or inherent – meanings.

The different interpretations of films provided by different audience members at different times are the result of changing social, political and economic conditions, as well as the viewers' constructed images of themselves; it isn't that there is a right or wrong interpretation. Staiger's method mixes historical research with ethnography in order to illustrate the specific reception of a film at a specific time. In *Perverse Spectators*, she analyses the reception of *Blonde Venus* (1932), starring Marlene Dietrich, through analysing a range of film journalism from the time it was released, as well as private diary entries and reminiscences of the audience members. Staiger's reception studies moves away from textual-led audience studies; but it is important to note that the film itself is still the focus of her work. Reception studies does not allow for endless interpretations of a film, but rather argues that there are a range of possible interpretations depending upon the audience's wider context. This identification of interpretations does, of course, require some sort of textual method, a way of reading the film; along with reception studies, Staiger also employs a range of post-structural approaches and a neo-formalist analysis. In doing this, Staiger – and other proponents of reception studies such as Annette Kuhn and Henry Jenkins – is able to counter the claim that discussion of the audience in film studies has moved too far away from the film itself, that in trying to address the gap where the audience should have been in film studies theorists have instead taken the opposite path – ignoring the film itself.

The development of audience theory in film studies can be seen as the shift between conceptualizing meaning as being inside the film form to arguing that it is the audience's encounter with the film which creates meaning. In moving between these two points, film studies has been influenced by psychoanalytic theory and cultural studies in order to try to construct an overview of the different ways in which films affect an audience, and vice versa.

Summary

- Film studies has traditionally believed that meaning is created within the text rather than through the interaction of audience and text.
- Psychoanalysis was initially the dominant approach to discussing the spectator, arguing that the spectator was positioned by the film.
- Star studies as an offshoot of spectatorship theory demonstrated how the audience's wider experiences contribute to the creation of meaning in a film.
- Audience studies in film theory has been influenced by cultural studies, leading to the use of ethnographic research and reception studies.
- The different approaches to the study of the audience of film have been accused of either ignoring the specific experiences of particular audience members or of ignoring the specific characteristics of individual films.

References and further reading

Andrew, D. (1984) *Concepts in Film Theory*, Oxford University Press, Oxford

Dayan, D. (1974) 'The Tutor code of classical cinema', *Film Quarterly*, vol 28, no 1, pp22–31

Dyer, R. (1979) *Stars*, British Film Institute, London

Ellis, J. (1982) *Visible Fictions: Cinema, Television, Video*, Routledge, London

Gormley, P. (2005) *The New Brutality Film: Race and Affect in Contemporary Hollywood Cinema*, Intellect Books, Bristol

Hall, S. (1980) 'Encoding and decoding', in S. Hall, D. Hobson, A. Lowe and P. Willis (eds) *Culture, Media, Language: Working Papers in Cultural Studies*, Hutchinson, London

Heath, S. (1978) 'Notes on suture', *Screen*, vol 18, pp189–196

Jancovich, M. and Faire, L. with Stubbings, S. (2003) *The Place of the Audience: Cultural Geographies and Film Consumption*, British Film Institute, London

Shaviro, S. (1993) *The Cinematic Body*, University of Minnesota Press, Minneapolis, MN

Stacey, J. (1993) *Stargazing: Hollywood Cinema and Female Spectatorship*, Routledge, London

Staiger, J. (2000) *Perverse Spectators: The Practices of Film Reception*, New York University Press, New York, NY

Young, A. (2010) *The Scene of Violence: Cinema Crime Affect*, Routledge, London

In *Media Reception Studies* (New York University Press, 2005), Janet Staiger provides a history of the different ways in which social scientific, linguistic and cultural studies approaches to film and television have discussed the relationship between the media and the audience.

For examples of affect theory, see Alison Young's *The Scene of Violence: Cinema, Crime, Affect* (Routledge, 2010), which develops the theory of criminological aesthetics, and Paul Gormley's *The New Brutality Film: Race and Affect in Contemporary Hollywood Cinema* (Intellect Books, 2005).

Henry Jenkins's research on film reception and consumption includes an analysis of fan cultures: *Textual Poachers: Television Fans and Participatory Culture* (Routledge, 1992).

PART IV

FILM AS A CONTEMPORARY DISCIPLINE

9

Creative Engagement

In this chapter we will consider:

- What are the creative aspects of film studies?
- How is creative work assessed?
- What is the relationship between theory and practice within the discipline?
- How has creative work changed the study of film?

The study of film as an academic subject was initially more concerned with the theoretical side of the subject, perhaps reflecting anxieties over making the subject seem sufficiently rigorous and academic. The creative aspects of studying film were marginalized, for fear of rendering the subject 'vocational' rather than 'academic'; degree courses tended to focus on film theory and critical response. The expansion of higher education has occurred alongside the proliferation of film-related courses, with an accompanying growth of confidence within the subject as it has gained academic maturity. One consequence of this has been the enormous diversity of courses available, offering the possibility of specializing in the creative aspects of film, or merely opting to study creative skills alongside the more traditional theoretical aspects of the subject. There is an enormous breadth of choice available.

It could be argued that there is no better way of understanding an art form than actually attempting to create your own piece of work. By working within the disciplines of screenwriting and film production, you are forced to experience the creative process, with its many problems, including the challenges of team work and communication. This will entail inevitable compromises as you attempt to realize your artistic vision within the context of time constraints, audience, resources and the demands of assessment criteria.

By endeavouring to create your own production piece, you are forced to consider all aspects of the film text: the shot and the edit, the *mise en scène* and the casting, the structure and the sound. The reality of creating a film text is complex and can be fraught with various problems. The skills which are required are not merely technical or artistic, but far-reaching skills, including the ability to communicate effectively, to work as part of a team, needing to be organized and focused, yet making optimal use of the resources available to you.

You may well have been involved in film-making in your studies – or leisure time – already; indeed, digital technology makes it easy for us all to be film-makers, even if you only have access to a mobile phone. The internet facilitates sharing of creative work, using social networking and blogging as possible tools for publicity and distribution.

Creativity

Film-making can appear to be a very romantic pursuit – from a distance – associated with notions of the director as artist, nurturing their vision and creativity. The figure of the auteur is very much embedded in the popular consciousness of the art of film-making. Yet the reality of film-making as part of your course will inevitably mean that artistic vision will be compromised by various constraints. As a result, you will need to be as realistic as possible in planning your project, although this does not mean that there is no space for creativity, as it can be the key to success.

The *Oxford English Dictionary* defines 'creative' as being 'inventive, imaginative, showing imagination as well as routine skill'. The central objective of any production work should ideally be to combine imagination and skill; but the idea of inventiveness also evokes the necessity of making original use of the resources at your disposal.

Nevertheless, creativity is not something arcane and mystical which will strike you at an opportune moment in a blinding flash of inspiration. Creativity is something that can be developed with hard work. Ideas for narrative, style, characters, themes, a striking shot or use of soundtrack can be found in a variety of sources. Your production work should grow organically out of your study of film. Your inspiration may come from other art forms: music, books, a news story or a photograph, for example. The best film-makers will exploit their influences, and yet be open to the vision and ideas of others. Alfred Hitchcock is one of the foremost auteurs in the history of film, yet his genius was the ability to realize his vision by appropriating the potential of those he worked with, such as the musical compositions of Bernard Herrmann.

Screenwriting

Screenwriting, or scriptwriting, may form part of your study of film-making, or you may opt to specialize in this area. As an art form, it lies at the interface of English and film studies, involving, as it does, the use of written English to evoke character, setting and construct narrative. Indeed, it is sometimes taught as part of creative writing courses within an English department. Nevertheless, the central drive of the screenplay is to use written language to evoke a visual medium, providing the raw material for the director and cinematographer to translate into the moving image. The screenplay needs to foreground action and description, rather than make the common error of being too dialogue-heavy. The screenplay should aim to summon up the film in the mind of the reader.

Even though creativity is the basis of a successful screenplay, it needs to be informed by an understanding of purpose and context. The screenplay is not the end result of the creative process, unlike a novel or poem, for example, but is a planning tool. It is written for specific audiences, for example as a business proposition to 'sell' the film to a studio, financier or production company. It is also a working document for the director and other key creative personnel to work with, adapt and use as the basis for a storyboard and shooting script. Its role as a planning tool means that the screenplay is in constant flux, needing to be revised to reflect the needs of other interested parties. Film-making is a collaborative process, meaning that your initial creative vision has to be adapted to incorporate the input of others. In the film industry, the script will go through numerous drafts.

There is no better way of appreciating the conventions of screenwriting than reading as many examples as possible. You will develop an understanding of the formal rules as well as an appreciation of creative possibilities. There are many books available which give advice on screenwriting, often suggesting certain rules and formulae for success. One of the oracles of the screenwriting industry, Robert McKee, argues that the secret to a successful screenplay is the story. Even though film-making is a collaborative process, for McKee the screenwriter is the one with the artistic vision, as all the other people involved – including the director – merely interpret the screenwriter's vision (see http://mckeestory.com/?page_id = 30).

Film-making

Although creativity and all that it entails is crucial to the production process, there is a fundamental requirement for the technical skills which will allow you to realize your vision. There is no getting around the fact that these skills will need to be learned, and that the best production work will demonstrate a flair and sophistication in applying the practical expertise involved in film-making. Production work is essentially a collaborative activity, which may involve a certain fluidity between the technical responsibilities of different members of the team, or may be organized so that each person has a specific responsibility. Nevertheless, any introduction to film-making should enable you to learn about all the different roles and the corresponding technical skills involved, so that even if you have no interest in lighting or sound recording, you are aware of the possibilities and able to assist where needed.

Hands-on learning about the technical aspects of film-making is one of the most valuable ways in which the production work can inform your study of film and your response to film texts. You will gain an awareness and insight, which is that of a practitioner, as well as a spectator and critic. This is a two-way process, though, as your decisions as a film-maker should be informed by the style and form of the films you have studied.

The secret to successful production work is the pre-production period, during which all the planning should take place. The director of a production would work closely with the director of photography to produce a storyboard and shooting script which will plan out the detail of the camera-work, lighting and *mise en scène*. No films – including documentaries – are made without extensive and painstaking preparation beforehand. This planning should allow you to take stock of what resources are needed, particularly in terms of technology, as well as allowing for the constraints of time and budget.

Planning the filming of each scene will translate the script into the shot sizes and camera movement required. These choices will be informed by an understanding of how different shot sizes and use of movement have a distinctive effect, allowing you to put into practice what you have learned from close analysis of film sequences. The design of the camerawork is crucial in allowing you to create the intended effect on the spectator, in terms of emotional response and developing the narrative.

At this stage of the planning process there will be three key planning documents:

1 *Script:* a written description of the film, including dialogue, settings, character descriptions and actions. This provides the initial guidance for the director. The script has its own distinctive rules in terms of formatting and layout, which are for ease of use and accessibility.
2 *Shooting script:* the original script with the addition of camera directions – essentially, the director's vision of the shooting of the film.
3 *Storyboard:* a visualization of what the final film will look like, using drawings, frame by frame, to illustrate the action, accompanied by written information regarding the shot sizes, action, lighting and camera movement. The preparation of a storyboard can save a lot of time, ultimately, as it will involve discussion of every shot, helping to highlight possible problems and to clarify ideas. The storyboard will be consulted throughout the production process, even though the film itself will evolve to reflect new ideas.

Your film-making should be informed by your study of film elsewhere on the course, as you will need to demonstrate your knowledge of narrative and genre conventions, as well as your understanding of the potential of film language. Nevertheless, this should not restrict your creativity. Really good film-makers will be confident enough with the conventions of film-making to make them their own, taking risks and even breaking the rules in order to communicate their vision in a style which is theirs alone.

Perhaps your most important consideration is the role of the audience in the film-making process. Film is a means of communication and therefore needs to engage its audience. You will need to have a clearly defined idea of who your audience is and the intended impact of your film. This should be fundamental to the very structure of the piece – its use of narrative and genre conventions – as well as to the detail of film style.

The production process will require good interpersonal skills as much as technical know-how. It is very important that you communicate clearly and regularly together as a group, and that everyone is confident about their role and what is expected of them in terms of commitment. It may well be that you will be working with some people for the first time, so it is important to be highly organized and have a professional working relationship in terms of clear expectations, good lines of communication and excellent pre-production planning to help clarify roles. The shooting of the film should be the least time-consuming part of the process, given all the preparation beforehand.

As with all stages of the production process, the shooting of the film requires careful attention to detail and thorough organizational skills. It is a very intensive time, requiring a clear schedule and organization of resources. A record needs to be kept of all the shots for future reference, and someone will need to take responsibility for continuity. All footage should be reviewed regularly during the process to ensure that there have been no problems, paying particular attention to the quality of sound, which can often detract from the overall production if not recorded effectively.

It is important not to overlook the creativity and technical expertise required to ensure that sound is used effectively in your production. Film is thought of primarily as a visual medium; yet sound can be integral to creating the desired impact and emotional resonance. The process of recording dialogue clearly can be technically challenging, requiring astute planning and expertise in using recording equipment. But sound is about much more than dialogue, encompassing sound effects, ambient sound, voiceover and music. All of these aspects of sound help to create the narrative and style of the film, needing to demonstrate your understanding of film form and conventions alongside your creativity. Some of the sound will be diegetic – captured during the production process – while non-diegetic sound (music and voice over) and sound effects will be added during editing.

The role of editor demands perseverance, communication skills, excellent computer skills and creativity. Editing has been referred to as a form of alchemy, with the editor taking the raw material of the film footage and sound, and arranging it to create the film narrative. The editor needs to have an excellent understanding of narrative, a sense of timing and rhythm, as well as excellent aesthetic awareness. Editing is about more than choosing the right shots and putting them into order; it is about creating meaning and resonance through the timing and symbolism of the edit. The director Stanley Kubrick believed that editing is the only unique aspect of 'cinematic art . . . It shares no connection with any other art form: writing, acting, photography, things that are major aspects of the cinema, are still not unique to it, but editing is' (Houston and Strick, 1972).

Assessment: Reflection and evaluation

A key part of creative work is the process of reflection and evaluation upon your work. Students are expected to reflect on their experience of practice, to analyse their completed production and to place their work in a historical and theoretical context. This requires you to reflect on how your studies have informed your work in terms of the films and theory you have covered during your course. Of course, your initial intentions for your work may not have been fully realized – either deliberately or inadvertently – but it is important to discuss such departures within a critical framework, demonstrating your understanding of the production process, industrial constraints, and issues regarding creativity and film conventions. Audience feedback can provide useful insights which can guide your process of reflection and allow you to consider a more objective viewpoint of something with which you have been so intimately involved.

An ethos of critical engagement and reflective analysis is embedded in most film courses, encouraging an approach to creative work which is based on dialogue and openness to feedback from others. The film industry is about collaboration, whether you are writing a screenplay or working as part of a production team in making a film. Preparation for creative work will cultivate your ability to respond constructively to the work of others, and the crucial ability to reflect on feedback you have received and to adapt your work accordingly.

A key aspect of the creative content of film courses is the requirement to evaluate your work. This reflective analysis should build on the theoretical content of your course in constructing an informed evaluation of your aims, the production process and the final artefact. Such analysis explicitly pulls together the practical and the theoretical aspects of the course, encouraging you to make connections between the two and to evaluate your own practice.

The assessment of your work will be based on an interplay between creativity and technical flair. Assessment may focus on:

- demonstration of professional practice;
- understanding and application of film form (structure, flow, organization of content, appropriate narrative and genre conventions);
- understanding of relevant theoretical debates as implicit in your development of the artefact;
- technical expertise.

Summary

- Creative work has become an increasingly important aspect of many film courses.
- Film studies courses can offer a vast array of options for creative work.
- All creative work requires a balance of creativity with technical expertise.
- Film production and screenwriting is about the ability to collaborate, as well as creative skills.
- All creative work is informed by the theoretical content of the course.
- Creative work requires the ability to reflect and evaluate analytically.

References and further reading

Houston, P. and Strick, P. (1972) 'Interview with Stanley Kubrick regarding *A Clockwork Orange*', *Sight and Sound*, spring

There are many books available which give advice about film production and screenwriting, and there are also some useful websites. A very comprehensive guide to film-making is Jane Barnwell's *The Fundamentals of Film-Making* (AVA Academia, 2008).

A classic text on film-making, written by the director of *The Ladykillers* and often cited as being the most influential text on the subject, is Alexander Mackendrick's *On Film Making* (Faber and Faber, 2006). Mackendrick became an esteemed teacher of film-making at the California Institute of the Arts, and the book incorporates his teaching notes.

There are a plethora of helpful guides to screenwriting, perhaps the most well known being Robert McKee's *Story: Substance, Structure, Style and the Principles of Screenwriting* (Methuen, 1999).

A couple of really useful websites which give plenty of advice and have many useful links are:

- http://www.bbc.co.uk/filmnetwork/filmmaking/guide/before-you-start/links-training
- http://www.creativeskillset.org/film/.

10

Film and Identity

In this chapter we will consider:

- How is film involved in national identity?
- How useful is it to consider national cinema?
- What impact has Hollywood had upon national cinema?
- What is the significance of world cinema studies?

Our everyday experience of cinema is dominated by Hollywood, when we consider the funding and origin of the films which are most readily available to us. Much the same could be said for film audiences in many other parts of the world, Hollywood having built a global presence which has been sustained for much of the history of film. Nevertheless, the Hollywood film industry has had to work to establish itself, and was not always predominant. You may be aware of other 'national' cinemas, such as British film and, even further afield, films which are not made in the English language.

Many national cinemas have struggled to survive in competition with the brand of Hollywood, contributing to widespread concerns that Hollywood is too powerful, that it works to extend American influence around the world, eroding the identity and culture of individual nations who are too weak to resist Hollywood's persuasive and slick marketing. Certainly, the rise of Hollywood has very much tracked the rise of America as a global power, and has even been argued to contribute to its economic and political status, perpetuating American values and ideologies. The academic study of film has always looked beyond Hollywood, recognizing national cinemas which have made significant contributions to film style and history, such as the neo-realist movement in 1940s Italy or the French New Wave. Nevertheless, as has been explored in earlier chapters, Hollywood has very much been at the centre of the academic discipline of film studies, dominating the canon.

Defining national cinema

The interpretation of exactly what 'national' cinema means has been the subject of much debate, involving a range of defining factors such as the nationality of the funding, the director/production team, the casting, the locations, and even the themes and subject matter of the film. As far back as the 1920s, the British government was concerned about the need to protect the British film industry from the US, arguing that the film industry was a vital component of national culture. The Cinematography Films Act of 1927 set out to combat this by setting a minimum quota of British films which must be shown by every exhibitor. In this case, a 'British' film was one that was made by a British subject or company, shot within the British Empire, and at least 75 per cent of labour costs must be paid to British citizens. In addition, the 'scenario' had to be written by a British citizen.

There have been many different policy attempts to defend the British film industry since the Cinematography Films Act, which have reflected changing attitudes towards the concept of national identity and the contribution made by cultural forms such as cinema. Attempts to nurture national cinema can be compromised by broader political factors, such as international relations and trade agreements, as was the case with the revision of the act in 1938, when a compromise was reached regarding the quota system in order to attract American funding into the UK to support the British film industry. One consequence of this was to encourage American companies to set up production units in the UK rather than encouraging a national film industry which was independent of foreign control. The importance accorded to cinema in contributing to national identity can be compromised by financial and political considerations, which more often than not further the interests of the dominant power: in this case, the US and Hollywood.

The factors which were cited as necessary to distinguish a film as British during the 1920s indicate how complex the issue of national cinema can be.

Legislation may be passed in order to support a film industry, but needs to be highly specific as to what the criteria are for a 'national' film. These factors can provide guidance for the process of labelling films and distinguishing between different national cinemas for the purpose of marketing or studying film. The discussion of the significance of nationality to cinema has evolved in the course of the academic study of film, reflecting broader theoretical concerns which have informed a broad range of disciplines.

The problem of the nation

Prior to the 1980s, the idea of national cinemas was very simple and straight-forward, based around the concept of the reflectionist nature of a national cinema. This concept assumes that cinema reflects the essence of the nation in terms of themes, subject matter, characters and landscapes. For example, the post-war Ealing comedies were held to define the spirit of the nation, with narratives of resistance to bureaucracy and change which could be ascribed to British defiance and community spirit in the wake of World War II. The academic Stephen Crofts describes the reflectionist view as constructing 'the homogenizing fictions of nationalism', contributing to generalized represen-tations of national cultures (Crofts, 1998, p386). These fictions are merely representations of aspects of a national culture, which vary according to his-torical and political context, and which will – inevitably – omit or even con-ceal aspects of a nation. They do not – and cannot – represent the reality of national culture, but may tend to repeat certain aspects of the national, creat-ing a mythical representation of Britishness, as with the Ealing comedies. A film such as *Passport to Pimlico* (1949) celebrates the community spirit and Dunkirk mentality of wartime through the story of a London neighbour-hood which decides to become an independent state following the discovery of treasure and historical relics.

The certainties and assumptions underlying the concept of national identity were increasingly questioned during the 1980s and 1990s, leading to new directions in the study of cinemas outside Hollywood. It was argued that nation states are essentially 'imagined communities' – a construction which cannot represent the complexity of the actual nation in all its diversity. This concept is particularly resonant regarding film, as it argues that national identity is based on shared images, stories and ideas which *forge* a sense of national culture. This implies a sense of community and common ideology which may be imagined, rather than real, given the complexity of actual 'communities'.

117

The problem of Hollywood

The US was just one of several countries which led the way in the early decades of film history, with the UK, France, Germany, Italy and Denmark making important contributions. The very nature of silent cinema meant that language was no impediment to distribution, with films being globally distributed, making it a borderless industry in terms of its audience. Early shorts were freely copied by other film-makers in this period, with little respect for national borders (or copyright), as the industry played with formats and sought out new attractions for their audiences. One example of this is *L'Arroseur Arrosée* (*The Waterer Watered*), often cited as the first film comedy, made in France by the Lumière brothers in 1895, and then extensively copied both within France and in the US.

The fact that the US was not a dominant force in the early years of film may come as a surprise to some, given that the history of film can seem to be predominantly a history of Hollywood, foregrounding the contribution of American film-makers. World history was to have a decisive impact upon the history of world cinemas, as the end of World War I marked the emergence of the American cinema as the dominant film-making industry, which it continues to be to this day. The European film industries had ground to a halt with the onset of hostilities, while Hollywood continued production, having a virtual monopoly with its home market, placing it in an ideal position to capitalize on the dearth of European product once the war was over.

American films could be made on a bigger budget, the costs being recouped by the homeland market, allowing product to be sold cheaply abroad to make a profit for the American studios, but simultaneously undermining the ability of national cinemas to recoup their costs. Competing national cinemas were largely unable to match the budget of American films and would therefore fail to attract the audiences, who developed a taste for the glamour and spectacle of Hollywood. Outside the US, it would come to be the case that it was cheaper to buy Hollywood product than to actually produce films themselves – a situation that remains to this day. On the other hand, some film-making nations were effectively isolated, leading to distinctive local developments independent of Hollywood in countries such as Germany, Sweden and Russia.

The 1920s saw Hollywood consolidate the studio system, producing films on an industrial scale, using the star system to develop slick marketing techniques, thus raising its game above any potential competitors. For national cinemas outside Hollywood, it was the start of a new era in which they faced the perennial dilemma of resisting Hollywood and nurturing their own film industry, a situation which continues to be of concern to this day. Some national film industries endeavoured to compete by emulating the Hollywood studio system and Hollywood film form, although struggling to match its budget and market stronghold. Yet there were examples of countries where film-making thrived, developing a distinctive style and cultural specificity. One example was the Japanese film industry, which prospered, producing more films than any other country by the late 1920s. Its feature films and viewing experience were influenced by Japanese theatre, commanding a greater audience share in Japan than Hollywood product.

National cinemas thrived in some areas of the globe despite the power of Hollywood. By the mid-1950s, only 35 per cent of feature films were made in the US and western Europe, the rest coming from countries such as Japan, Indian, Mexico and other developing nations (Thompson and Bordwell, 1994, p459). Hollywood had cut back its output during the 1950s, yet cinema audiences were expanding to match the pace of industrialization in these countries, creating an appetite for film which powered the indigenous film industries. Television had failed to establish itself to the extent that it had in the West, and there was a real appetite for films featuring the music, stars and culture to which the indigenous population could relate.

Third World theory

Film theory tended to centre on Hollywood cinema, although the critical contributions of French and British theorists helped to establish some status for the film industries in those countries. The critical ferment of the 1960s and 1970s saw the emergence of the concept of Third World cinema, which called for an indigenous film industry in developing countries which would break away from Hollywood conventions. Theorists responded to the fragmentation of the old empires and the growing independence movement in former colonies by arguing for a new cinema which rejected Hollywood classical cinematic conventions, associated with American values. They argued for an imperfect cinema which would give expression to national themes in a distinctive national style. The former colonies could not hope to have an infrastructure or budget to match Hollywood; but this could be an advantage in developing a distinctive style. It was argued that Third World film should aim to confront, agitate and empower the indigenous audience, helping to construct a sense of national pride through a distinctive national culture.

Third World film-makers and theorists were influenced by the creative and ideological possibilities of film movements such as Italian neo-realism and

Soviet montage, where film form is tailored to reflect social and political concerns. Italian neo-realism was particularly influential in Latin American countries, cited as a role model for a cinema which expresses the experiences of the poor using documentary realism, and making a virtue of its technical shortcomings, given the lack of resources.

Third World film theory was an attempt to recognize the potential of other cinemas, but was increasingly questioned as a viable critical approach. It was seen to be flawed in terms of advocating a uniform approach for different national cinemas rather than distinctive indigenous styles of film-making. In advocating a deliberately 'imperfect' film style, theorists overlooked the importance of spectatorial pleasure, which would help to build an audience in competition with the pleasures of Hollywood. Robert Stam describes such cinema as offering 'miserabilist exoticism' where film-makers must speak for the oppressed (Stam, 2000, p283).

Post-colonialism

Post-colonialism at its simplest level is a revision of the ideas at the core of Third World theory, which proved to be of limited usefulness in recognizing the complexity of cinema produced outside Hollywood. Post-colonial theory emerged in the course of the 1980s, offering a new perspective on cinema produced by developing countries. The context for this theory was an engagement with a new world order in which the ex-colonies struggled to assert their own national identity, independent of their former colonizers and the dominant world powers.

Post-colonialism is a complex set of theories, covering a diversity of critical approaches and ideas. At the heart of this lies a central concern with the 'cultural interaction between colonizing powers and the societies they colonized, and the traces that this interaction left on the ... arts' (Bahri and Vasudeva, 1996, pp137–138). Cultural identity is recognized as being increasingly hybrid in the era of globalization, and therefore more complex, not simply a divide between the colonizers and the colonized. Film is just one aspect of culture both within the developed and the developing worlds which can articulate the themes and narratives of the post-colonial era. One key theme is the issue of multiple identities, alongside 'the geographical displacements characteristic of the post-independence era' (Stam, 2000, p295). The consideration of identity is informed by ethnicity, but is inevitably extended to consider the implications regarding gender, sexuality and religion.

A film such as Gurinder Chadha's *Bhaji on the Beach* (1994) lends itself to a post-colonial reading. It tells the story of a daytrip to Blackpool for a diverse group of British Asian women, representing the chasms within a single community regarding attitudes to race, age and gender. They are united in the face of racism yet divided by generational attitudes to traditional values. The entrenched attitudes of the older generation of women who cling steadfastly to tradition are contrasted with the enlightened sophistication of a relative on a visit from Bombay. The film can be described as post-colonial in dealing with the diverse issues regarding identity among the Asian community established in the UK. The film has been cited as typical of the 'diasporic cinema' of the 1990s and 2000s, which 'represented a diverse thematic strand of filmmaking, concerned with the varied cultural experiences of second- and third-generation migrants' (Grainge et al, 2007, p555).

Post-colonialism initiated new debates around nationality and identity, yet met with criticism for various shortcomings, including its failure to engage with the political and economic dimensions, especially given the economic forces which drive globalization.

The transnational

The concept of the 'transnational' dominates consideration of identity and nationality in contemporary film studies. 'Transnationality' covers a range of debates and issues regarding identity and the complexities of globalization, building on aspects of post-colonialism and Third World theory. This theoretical context considers the impact upon cinema of the 'accelerating transnational flows of people (tourists, immigrants, exiles, refugees, guest workers), of technology . . . of finance and media images . . . and of ideologies (such as the global spread of western rhetorics of democracy)' (Crofts, 1998, p386). Film producers are increasingly concerned with appealing to a global audience, spanning multiple nationalities, and the diversity of peoples within each state.

One concern about the growing global nature of cinema audiences is that this may lead to greater homogeneity in terms of film style and content, a concern which was formerly associated with the dominance of Hollywood cinema. On the other hand, it may be argued that the need to appeal to more global audiences can lead to a more diverse cinema, as Hollywood seeks to embrace other cultures in terms of subject matter and casting, as well as working with film-making expertise from other nations. The production of the *Kung Fu Panda* series and films such as *The Karate Kid* (2010) are examples of Hollywood's determination to appeal to the Chinese audience, which is forecast to become the second biggest cinema market after the US. Epic films such as the *Harry Potter* and *The Lord of the Rings* series are produced with a global audience in mind.

The concept of a national cinema has been undermined to some extent by the growing trend for international co-productions, which can boost the budget and subsequent audience appeal of films. It could be argued that this can also lead to greater homogeneity of product, as the national specificity of a film will be compromised by the need to target more than one nationality. One of the major factors in the growth of co-productions during recent years has been the necessity for Hollywood to find new ways of meeting the growing costs of film production, as well as spreading the risk more widely. Hollywood majors have increasingly looked to cheaper overseas labour markets wherever possible, along with using overseas production facilities which could offer advantageous financial arrangements. Such cost-saving practices are typical of the wider industrial practices beyond film production within the context of globalization. It could be argued that Hollywood is simply exploiting cheaper overseas opportunities in order to maintain its dominant position, thus perpetuating its status as a colonizing power. On the other hand, whereas the centre of power for the film industry still resides in Hollywood, individual films can often be seen to be the consequence of transnational cultural and industrial practices. Perhaps it is not merely the case that Hollywood uses its position as a global entertainer to perpetuate American culture and ideology, as have been the accusations of those critical of American 'cultural imperialism'.

Theorists have argued that the concept of national cinema has limited usefulness, believing that the fixation with the national overlooks the local, as well as the growing importance of the transnational. Local communities within nation states have used film as a means to gain visibility and to enunciate a sense of identity, as with Native American film-making in the US or Welsh-language cinema within the UK. The growth in the trend of co-productions and the popularity of world cinema, enhanced by the burgeoning film festival circuit and ready availability on DVD, has been cited as evidence of 'borderless' cinema. Yet cinema continues to be labelled by nationality outside a still-dominant Hollywood.

Even when a seemingly culturally specific cinema is identified, it can still be judged to be indebted to Hollywood. Pedro Almodovar's films have defined Spanish cinema during the past decades, vividly representing aspects of Spanish life, yet referencing and borrowing extensively from the

Hollywood melodrama, as in the film *All about My Mother* (1999). This can be seen as typical of how European/art cinema is enmeshed with Hollywood forms and traditions, 'rarely [sitting] in opposition to Hollywood but often emerged in creative dialogue with its forms and conventions, even as it culturally or stylistically reworked them' (Grainge et al, 2007, p553). What borders there are between national cinemas are porous, making the definition of specific cultural identity an academic activity in the face of widespread cultural osmosis.

The academic Andrew Higson has been a key contributor to debates regarding transnational film. He has argued that it can still be useful to consider films in terms of their nation of origin, as it is a method of classification 'in the complex debates about cinema' (Higson, 2006, p16). The recognition of national cinemas can also serve as a means of resisting the market dominance of Hollywood, giving a film a platform which it might not have received by attaching it to the notion of a national cinema. For Andrew Dix, the attribution of particular films to a nation 'may be enlivening', one reason being that 'it can identify a locus of cultural resistance to the directly colonial or otherwise hegemonic force of other states' (Dix, 2008, p288).

One recent example of this is the recognition accorded to Iranian cinema in recent years, the anti-western ideology of the fundamentalist regime having led to a flourishing national cinema. After the Khomeini Revolution in 1979, the Islamist regime largely prohibited western films and gave government support to its own film industry. The work of directors such as Abbas Kiarostami and Mohsen Makhmalbaf, as part of the so-called New Wave of Iranian cinema, has received great acclaim on the international festival circuit. Nevertheless, these directors have established an art cinema in Iran, which has not always met with government approval, in contrast to the more commercial Iranian cinema, which is largely unknown outside Iran. In the case of the New Wave of Iranian cinema, the films increasingly explored the plight of ordinary Iranians within the sociocultural context of modern-day Iran, a regime which has been the subject of intense opposition from the West, especially given the fundamentalist agenda.

Summary

- The study of film should consider issues around its importance as a cultural artefact in forming our sense of identity.
- National identity is an imagined concept, based on a shared culture, images, narratives and traditions.

123

- The debates around national identity and film have been centred on the power of Hollywood.
- Shifting global populations and the technological and economic impact of globalization have had an impact upon national cinemas.
- A national cinema can be considered vital to the identity of a nation state.
- Films, and how we consider films, have evolved to reflect the changing agenda regarding national identities.

References and further reading

Bahri, D. and Vasudeva, M. (1996) *Between The Lines: South Asians and Postcoloniality*, Temple University Press, Philadelphia, PA

Crofts, S. (1998) 'Concepts of national cinema', in J. Hill and P. C. Gibson (eds) *The Oxford Guide to Film Studies*, Oxford University Press, Oxford, pp385–394

Dix, A. (2008) *Beginning Film Studies*, Manchester University Press, Manchester

Grainge, P., Jancovitch, M. and Monteith, S. (2007) *Film Histories: An Introduction and Reader*, Edinburgh University Press, Edinburgh

Higson, A. (2006) 'The limiting imagination of national cinema', in E. Ezra and T. Rowden (eds) *Transnational Cinema: The Film Reader*, Routledge, London and New York, pp15–26

Stam, R. (2000) *Film Theory: An Introduction*, Blackwell, Malden, MA

Thompson, K. and Bordwell, D. (1994) *Film History: An Introduction*, McGraw-Hill, New York, NY

A really useful source for this topic is Stephen Crofts's chapter 'Concepts of national cinema' included in *The Oxford Guide to Film Studies*, edited by John Hill and Pamela Church Gibson (Oxford University Press, 1998). Also *The Oxford History to World Cinema*, edited by Geoffrey Nowell-Smith (Oxford University Press, 1996) offers a comprehensive guide to national cinemas.

11

Postmodernism and Cultural Studies

In this chapter we will:

- define postmodernism and evaluate its influence on film studies;
- look at postmodernism's contribution to aesthetic discussions of film;
- examine how postmodernism links to existing approaches in film studies, such as feminist theory.

While there is not one specifically postmodern film theory, postmodernism has certainly informed a range of ways of thinking about film and has therefore had a major impact upon the development of film studies. This is apparent in the way in which the concept of postmodernism has been used to analyse film production and film style, and to develop theoretical approaches. Postmodernism has influenced film studies in a number of ways. For some theorists, the advent of a postmodern aesthetic in film seemed to represent a break with the existing form of classical Hollywood film-making. Postmodernism's elevation of popular culture was part of a further erosion of the boundaries between high art and popular culture which had been central to the foundation of film studies. Its rejection of the dominant representations in, and responses to, popular culture led to an opening up of what kind of films were made and how they could be interpreted; this was particularly influential in feminist film theory and practice.

Postmodernism has proved to be a controversial concept, but one which has informed the discussion of the aesthetics of contemporary cinema and provided new approaches to issues of representation and audience. Post-modernism has been particularly influential in the development of film studies in its emphasis on pluralism. The idea that there are a plurality of meanings in and responses to film further encouraged the move away from the total theory approach of screen theory and structuralism. The influence of postmodernism was characteristic of film studies' assimilation of approaches developed in cultural studies, and reinforced the importance of the audience in analysing film.

In addition to being controversial, postmodernism is also an elusive concept which can be defined in different ways by different groups, and covers a range of theories and practices. The term postmodernism can be used to describe a period, an attitude, a mode of thought and even behaviour. There are postmodern works in architecture, literature, painting, theatre and across all forms of media, as well as film. According to different theorists, postmodernism is either a subversive view of the world expressed across a variety of forms or it is an ideologically conservative one. The inclusion of such a wide range of disciplines and ideas is partly what makes postmodernism difficult to define; but there are certain aesthetic characteristics which are generally agreed to constitute postmodernism. These include an emphasis on surface style and appearance, creating meaning through inter-textuality, such as in the continual reference to other films, and the use of *bricolage*, the mixing together of an eclectic mix of styles within one text. Postmodernism rejects boundaries and certainties, anything which relies on a unified and linear way of seeing the world. This includes grand theories or meta-narratives, which attempt to provide an explanation for how the world works, such as through religion, capitalism, communism, feminism and, probably most controversially, science. Postmodernism attacked the certainty expressed by these narratives as misplaced and doomed to failure; the world is a much more chaotic place than these approaches allow.

This rejection of unifying explanations of the world was a way of articulating an increasingly uncertain existence in which established roles and behaviour – such as gender expectations, the make-up of the family, the role of religion – were rapidly changing. Previous theoretical and artistic movements, such as modernism and structuralism, had also acknowledged the chaos and fragmentation that living in the modern world entailed. For modernism, this was personified by the apparent 'madness' of World War I and its annihilation of millions of people. The fundamental difference with post-modernism was that while modernists saw uncertainty and chaos as destructive characteristics, postmodernists celebrated these features of contemporary life. In this context, the questioning of the meta-narratives was a kind of liberation – everything was open to question and ways of living could be redefined. In this way, postmodernism is linked to post-structuralism as both are characterized by pluralism: the idea that there are multiple theories, readings and interpretations, rather than a homogeneous one. In film studies, this is similar to the developments in spectatorship and audience theory with the shift from the imaginary spectator to the recognition of the audience as a range of different individuals who constituted the mass, all with different experiences and identities (see Chapter 8 for further discussion of the development of spectatorship theory in film studies).

What is a postmodern film?

If definitions of postmodernism itself are contested, then it is not surprising that there are a variety of approaches apparent in discussing what is a post-modern film. These disagreements are often a result of the fact that some characteristics claimed as postmodern, such as inter-textuality, have been apparent in films from earlier periods. There is, though, broad agreement that postmodern film-making is characterized by the merger of previously sepa-rate genres and aesthetics, a fragmentation of linear narrative apparent in con-fusion around the period and setting of a film, the emphasis on style, spectacle, special effects and images over narrative causality, and the juxtaposition of previously distinct emotional tones. The mode of address of postmodern film is a knowingness and ironic commentary; an understanding that the audience has seen it all before and recognizes film's status as fabrication. Included in this definition of postmodern film-making was a wide range of different types of films made for different audiences, from mainstream blockbusters to art house cinema. Films such as *Blade Runner* (1982), *Back to the Future* (1985), *Who Framed Roger Rabbit?* (1988), *Raiders of the Lost Ark* (1984), *Blue Velvet* (1986) and *Raising Arizona* (1987) were all seen – in different ways – as exemplars of postmodernism.

The postmodernist political and social analysis of the world, as well as the art works associated with it, have been interpreted as both subversive and reactionary. In the arts and humanities, including film studies, there are com-peting claims for postmodernism as being either an oppositional form or part of mainstream culture. This debate has centred on whether postmod-ernist style is parody or pastiche. Developed by one of the most influential theorists – and critics – of postmodernism, Frederic Jameson (1984), the concepts of parody and pastiche were a way of demonstrating why

127

postmodernism, with its reliance on pastiche, was a conservative style. In this approach Jameson is continuing the ideological criticism found in screen theory, seeing the form of postmodern Hollywood cinema as ideologically conservative. In Jameson's distinction, pastiche is defined as a visually exciting imitation of existing styles which remains superficial because it is divorced from wider contexts, specifically a sense of history. It is this aspect of postmodern style which attracts accusations of form over content. In contrast, the oppositional mode – parody – is also imitative but aims to evaluate and subvert the original codes or meaning associated with the imitated form. The oppositional tendency questions and challenges, attempting to construct new meaning through placing existing cultural styles and movements in new contexts. In postmodern cinema, this could refer to the way in which the intertextual mixing of genres changes the meaning of the original representations (e.g. gender, ethnicity). The mainstream mode of pastiche is merely an imitation or copy with nothing new to say; Jameson termed this style of film production the 'nostalgia film'. In this analysis, the use of inter-textuality and emphasis on the look of the film in, for example, *Chinatown* (1974) and *Body Heat* (1981), means that they cannot recreate a 'real' past but merely repeat pre-existing representations of the past. The result of this is that the films lack any historical depth or political analysis.

Whether a text is parody or pastiche, they will share characteristics of style, form and content which operate within either the oppositional or mainstream mode. Predictably, the categorization of texts in these terms is open to debate. In his overview of postmodernist debates and film, John Hill puts forward some examples to demonstrate how the distinction between parody and pastiche could work in analysing Hollywood film: 'Robert Altman's *The Long Goodbye* (1973) quotes from film history and reworks genre conventions with obvious parodic intent – to debunk the myth of the private eye and the values he represents.' In contrast, Hill argues that *The Untouchables* (1987) is characterized by the use of pastiche 'in the clever, but politically and emotionally "blank", reconstruction of the Odessa Steps sequence from the revolutionary Russian film *Battleship Potemkin*, 1925' (Hill, 1998, p101).

The identification of the postmodern film led film studies in two main directions. In one approach, the films were examined for the ways in which they represented the experience of living in postmodernism. The second, more formalist-influenced approach centred on a debate over whether postmodern film-making constituted a break with classical Hollywood film-making. For example, *Back to the Future* was postmodernist in the way in which it focused on disruptions in time and space. Although the film itself is told through a conventional narrative, the subject of the plot – that it is possible to go back to the future – can be read as a postmodernist attack on linear causality and an attempt to represent the disorientation of living in the postmodern world. *Raiders of the Lost Ark*, another mainstream blockbuster, could be defined as postmodernist in its recycling of images and forms from the past, as seen in the repeated references to 1950s B-movies and old television series. *Blade Runner*'s dystopian themes and post-industrial city setting seemed to be a metaphor for postmodernism in which established certainties and ways of life were disappearing.

Postmodernism and post-classical film

Postmodern ideas have had a major influence on the historical poetic approach in film studies where the idea of challenging meta-narratives applied, in this case, to the characterization of Hollywood as having a single, homogeneous style. As discussed in Chapter 7 on narrative theory, historical poetics is an attempt to isolate the key characteristics of film-making from a particular time and place in order to construct an objective rather than interpretive reading of film. The most influential theorists in this area, whose work provides the foundation for many film studies courses, are David Bordwell and Kristin Thompson. In their books *The Classical Hollywood Cinema* (Bordwell et al, 1985) and *Film Art: An Introduction* (Bordwell and Thompson, 1990), they identified a series of aesthetic 'norms' dominant in Hollywood film which they defined as classical. These norms, they argued, were dominant from 1917 to 1960. Although this might suggest that there was a change in style after this date, Bordwell goes on to argue that apparent challenges to this homogeneous style, such as in the work of directors of the 'New Hollywood', including Francis Ford Coppola, Martin Scorsese and Terrence Malick, are, in fact, integrated within the dominant form – the unity of the classical storytelling form remains. In this analysis the stability and persistence of the film style is directly linked to the institution which produced it: the Hollywood studio system. This system was explicitly based on a factory model of mass production for greatest efficiency, an approach which was transferred to film style; classical narrative and genre conventions could work as a model to be reproduced, something which became known as a group style.

Critics of the idea that the classical Hollywood model has persisted unchanged point to the variations in institutional context since 1960, which, they argue, has shattered the group style and monolithic practice of the old studio system, and has resulted in a break with classical style. The postmodern film is the result of these changes; it is aesthetically different to the filmmaking of the studio era. These changes in the nature of storytelling – disrupted narrative, the eclectic mix of genres and tone – reflected wider shifts in contemporary society. Jameson (1984) identifies this shift as the 'cultural logic of late capitalism'. This is the result of the move from an economy based on production and manufacturing to one which is information-based and abstract, fuelled by the development of new technologies such as the internet. This shift from established traditions into completely new ways of working resulted in, postmodern critics argued, a disruption to established communities and social roles. This account of late capitalism is relevant to the Hollywood film industry, which has gone through similar changes. During the period of the classic studio system (1930s to 1960s), the five major and three minor studios were engaged solely in making films, and they were the controlling force in production, distribution and exhibition in the US, and were dominant worldwide. This system has been replaced by global conglomerates; the monolithic studio structure has been broken down into small corporations which distribute films across multiple platforms and are multimedia companies, rather than film producers. If, as historical poetics has argued, there is a direct link between style and institution, then this breakup of the system is likely to affect the style of films.

Henry Jenkins (1995), an influential theorist in historical poetics and reception studies, argues that while Bordwell's analysis of the endurance of the classical film style is broadly correct, he fails to acknowledge the extent of experimentation and disruption that has taken place in the decades since the 1960s. He argues that this break with classical film style happened so rapidly that it quickly became integrated within the dominant style and invisible to the viewer, but that it did change the previously dominant form: 'Over time these stylistic experiments get absorbed, so that the film remains fully comprehensible according to traditional classical criteria of causality, coherence and continuity, while adopting a range of stylistic options which would have been transgressive in the studio-era film making' (Jenkins, 1995, p116). Jenkins's analysis of post-classical cinema is, he states, also compatible with the postmodern analysis of wider cultural changes, but he prefers to use the term 'post classical film' to stress the link to the previous classical film style. In contrast to much of the postmodern analysis of contemporary Hollywood cinema, Jenkins does not want to cast evaluative judgement as to whether it is a radical political form or an empty superficial one; rather, he argues that the style itself must be clearly identified first. To do this there will need to be an analysis of the interconnection between the film, audience, institution and film-maker in order to understand how wider contexts may shape the changing film style.

Postmodernism and authorship

Auteur theory in film studies can be defined as an example of a meta-narrative. Auteur theory was an attempt to construct a total theory of film, a way of explaining how film was created and why it was important; it was the vision of an individual artist, their way of transmitting their view of the world. Auteur theory is also closely linked to the divide between high art and popular culture as it was a way of legitimizing the study of popular culture – film – by assigning an author and therefore re-categorizing film as an art form (see Chapter 1 for further discussion of the development of authorship in film studies). In the context of postmodernism, auteur theory stands for everything which postmodernism challenges. Auteur theory is about certainty in the way that once a director is identified as an auteur, they remain one; it is a hierarchical system based on categories and borders, and it uses the language of the divide between art forms, all aspects which postmodernism has attempted to question and disrupt. In addition, the postmodern aesthetic with its emphasis on collage and pastiche, of borrowing from pre-existing forms, would seem to be a shift away from the traditional idea of the creative individual responsible for the style and meaning in their work. The cultural studies theorist Dick Hebdige (1998) identified the way in which postmodernism's emphasis on borrowing and recycling of forms and images has the effect of challenging the value placed on originality and authenticity. The auteur is no longer expected to invent but rather to collect and rearrange previously existing forms. Given this, it would be expected that the influence of postmodernism on film studies would be to further erode the influence of authorship; but this has not necessarily been the case.

In his overview of postmodernism and film, John Hill (1998) questions the extent of the erosion of the border between originality and replication, high art and popular culture promised by postmodernism. The concept of authorship has, he argues, remained resilient. He uses the example of *Blue Velvet* to demonstrate this persistence. As a film, *Blue Velvet* displays all the characteristics of postmodernism: eclecticism, the mixing of avant-garde and popular conventions, its use of an ironic play with visual signifiers. In contrast, the marketing of the film and the critical and theoretical discussions around it have been in terms of the auteur, David Lynch. In his analysis of the films of

David Lynch, the film critic Jonathan Rosenbaum demonstrates how theories of authorship and postmodernism overlap. In discussing the development of Lynch's career, Rosenbaum (in Hoberman and Rosenbaum, 1991) contends that: 'You might say that as auteurism turned junk into art, postmodernism turns art into junk. Even when an original artist like Lynch appears, it's not long before he starts quoting himself, using his work in a postmodernist way.'

Postmodernism and gender studies: Queer theory

Postmodernism has had a profound influence on the development of feminist film theory, and the related areas of lesbian and gay criticism and gender studies. This influence is apparent in the changing way in which gender is discussed in film studies.

Feminist film theory introduced the idea of the gendered spectator into film studies in the 1970s, but was soon criticized for relying on an essentialist model of gender which saw male and female as homogeneous groups sharing the same characteristics. In postmodernism, this idea of the unified identity was replaced by the concept of multiple identities; rather than simply female, the spectator may be influenced by a range of factors to do with race, ethnicity, age, sexuality etc., any of which may be dominant at different periods. This conceptualization is typical of postmodernism's refusal to accept rigid boundaries, preferring instead to see gender as fluid, something which can be chosen and performed rather than innate. The challenge to the essentialist view of gender in feminist film theory led to the development of what the leading feminist theorist Annette Kuhn defines as 'micro narratives and micro histories of the fragmented female spectator' (Kuhn, 1994, p202), rather than the totalizing view of the female spectator found in apparatus theory.

This shift in feminist film theory has been influenced by the work of the sociologist Judith Butler (1990). Butler has argued that as gender is not natural but an ideological construction, then so is the way in which society understands biological difference. While it had become accepted to define gender as a constructed identity based on the expectations of a particular society at a particular time, Butler goes further and argues that this understanding of gender has affected the way in which a society divides people by biological difference as male and female. Butler accepts that there are biological differences, but points out that society has chosen to categorize individuals along those differences rather than any other. In order to provide evidence for this, she demonstrates how historically this was not always so and problematizes the binary definitions by pointing to the existence of a third category – hermaphrodite.

Butler's analysis forces us to question the validity of some of the most funda-mental categories – male and female – which we recognize in society. This analysis of gender has been influential in the development of queer theory, which subverts established definitions and categories to do with identity.

Queer was originally used as a term of abuse for gay men, but has now been 'reclaimed' by groups as a form of positive identification (it should be noted, though, that it is still a controversial term). In film theory and cultural studies, queer is not synonymous with gay, but instead questions such narrow definitions of sexuality and gender. Queer refers to people who identify as gay, lesbian, bisexual, transgender and intersex, but also has a wider meaning in referring to anyone who does not feel part of the mainstream heterosexual ('heteronormative') society. Queer theory has a close relationship to feminist theory and gender studies. It shares with those theorists an interest in studying non-normative expressions of gender and sexuality. Queer theory rejects the essentialist nature of theories of identity which are expressed through binary oppositions – male/female, gay/straight, etc. Queer theory argues that people do not simply categorize themselves in this way: representations don't con-form to either side of these divides – instead, there is another space outside of these oppositions and it is this space which is 'queer'.

Postmodernist film and queer

Like postmodernism itself, queer includes a diverse range of cultural prac-tices, theoretical approaches and behaviour. The intersection between theory and practice in queer is particularly notable with queer directors such as Todd Haynes (*I'm Not There*, 2007; *Far from Heaven*, 2002) and Gus van Sant (*Milk*, 2008; *My Own Private Idaho*, 1991) breaking down barriers between film-making, activism and theory. Queer cinema is compatible with post-modern style. It is characterized by an eclectic mix of style, from art cinema experimentalism to melodramatic excess. It borrows from a range of different genres and film history and, like postmodernism, embraces a wide range of production and audience contexts, from the Hollywood mainstream to inde-pendent film-makers speaking to a niche audience. Films such as *Brokeback Mountain* (2006) and the comedy *I Love You Phillip Morris* (2009) have been identified as queer in their subversion or 'queering' of genres (western, rom com and crime film). Tim Burton, particularly in his collaborations with Johnny Depp, has been described as a queer auteur due to the themes of alienation and sympathy for characters who do not conform to mainstream society's expectations (*Edward Scissorhands*, 1990; *Ed Wood*, 1994).

A queer film may not have an explicitly gay theme, but can be defined as queer once it has accumulated queer readings. Alexander Doty, whose work has been particularly influential in the development of queer theory, uses the concept of a queer space and applies it to a film made long before the development of queer theory: *Sylvia Scarlet* (1935). In this film, Katherine Hepburn, an actress whose star persona emphasized her unconventional gender characteristics (trousers, suit jackets, athleticism, strong features) plays a young woman who dresses as a man (Sylvester) in order to avoid arrest. Doty (1998) argues that this film is queer because straight male audience members who gain sexual pleasure from looking at Katherine Hepburn in male dress are having a queer moment – something which cannot be simply categorized as gay or straight.

This emphasis on audience response in queer theory further continues the momentum in film studies away from the analysis of the text as bearer of meaning to finding the meaning in the audience. In the context of queer theory, the concept of the audience and the construction of meaning has been taken to an extreme, completely rejecting the idea of the homogeneous spectator. Now the audience is conceived of as not only being made up of a range of individuals with specific experiences which make them different from each other; each spectator is also made up of fragmented, even contradictory identities, and any one of these can be dominant at different periods while watching a film. In this model, the film itself can be appropriated and read in different ways – as queer, as straight, as radical or as conservative; there is no longer a fixed meaning for the audience to uncover.

Postmodernism has been influential in a variety of ways in film studies and this has tended to be a product of postmodernism's challenge to established ways of theorizing about film. In a variety of aspects of film studies, such as authorship, feminist film theory and historical poetics, postmodernism has challenged an established meta-narrative, resulting in a pluralist approach to understanding film style and meaning.

Summary

- Postmodernism is a wide-ranging term and relates to a variety of political, philosophical and artistic movements in both theory and practice.
- In film, postmodernism has become synonymous with an eclectic mix of styles and tones, which for many theorists is indicative of a superficiality and lack of seriousness.

- The postmodernist attack on the divide between high art and popular culture is related to film studies' defence of cinema as worthy of academic study.
- Influential theoretical approaches in film studies, such as auteur theory and feminist film theory, can be seen as examples of meta-narratives which postmodernism challenged.

Reference and further reading

Bordwell, D. and Thompson, K. (1990) *Film Art: An Introduction*, McGraw-Hill, New York, NY

Bordwell, D., Staiger, J. and Thompson, K. (1985) *The Classical Hollywood Cinema: Film Style and Mode of Production to 1960*, Routledge, London

Butler, J. (1990) *Gender Trouble*, Routledge, London

Doty, A. (1998) 'There's something queer here', in A. Doty (ed) *Out in Culture: Gay, Lesbian and Queer Essays on Popular Culture*, Duke University Press, Durham, NC

Hebdidge, D. (1988) *Hiding in the Light*, Routledge, London

Hill, J. (1998) 'Film and postmodernism', in P. C. J. Hill (ed) *The Oxford Guide to Film Studies*, Oxford University Press, Oxford, pp96–104

Hoberman, J. and Rosenbaum, J. (1991) *Midnight Movies*, De Capo Press, New York, NY

Jameson, F. (1984) *Postmodernism, or the Cultural Logic of Late Capitalism*, Duke University Press, Durham, NC

Jenkins, H. (1995) 'Historical poetics', in M. J. J. Hollows (ed) *Approaches to Popular Film*, Manchester University Press, Manchester, pp99–121

Kuhn, A. (1994) *Women's Pictures*, Verso, London

Dominic Strinati provides a comprehensive overview of postmodern style across the media in 'Postmodernism and popular culture' in *An Introduction to the Theories of Popular Culture* (Routledge, 1995).

Andreas Huyssen's *After the Great Divide: Modernism, Mass Culture and Postmodernism* (Macmillan, 1986) is a major theoretical work which discusses the antagonistic relationship between high art and mass culture through music, painting and cinema.

In addition to Alexander Doty's analysis of queer cinema, *Out in Culture: Gay, Lesbian and Queer Essays on Popular Culture* (Duke University Press, 1998), see also Harry M. Benshoff's *Monsters in the Closet* (Manchester University Press, 1997), which applies queer readings to the horror genre.

12

Film as Industry

In this chapter we will consider:

- What is meant by a 'film industry'?
- Why is it important to consider the industrial context of film?
- What is the impact of new technology upon film-making and exhibition?

The emphasis on textual analysis and auteur theory in the development of film studies as a discipline has meant that a major aspect of film, its industrial, business and technological context, has been sidelined, even ignored. Until relatively recently, this gap has persisted, creating what Richard Dyer has referred to as the discipline's 'guilty conscience'. This guilty conscience was expressed in the feeling that 'students of film "ought to talk about the industry"' (Dyer, 1998, p9). This sense of duty without the methodological foundations for examining the new area led, Dyer argues, to unsophisticated descriptions of the film industry which did not have the academic rigour of other areas of film studies. It is through the integration of approaches from cultural studies, history and the social sciences that film studies has been able to analyse the relationship of the film to the industry which produced it in a more productive way.

Art and business

One of the reasons that film studies as a discipline initially resisted the study of the film industry was due to the subject's placement within the schools of arts and humanities, rather than the social sciences. This was consistent with the disciplinary aim of establishing film as an art form, as a serious subject worthy of study in the same way that literature and fine art were. The definition of film as an art form with an author would not be easily compatible with the study of film as an industrial form, where film is the product of many individuals working within a business context. The profit motive associated with the film industry – particularly Hollywood – was also problematic as art is traditionally conceived of as existing outside of economic constraints.

The 'guilty conscience' of film studies was a product of the discipline's limited development of the type of skills needed to analyse the film industry, such as economic and historical methods, due to the bias towards analytical and evaluative approaches. Film studies was, in fact, explicit in defining itself as an analytical subject, in opposition to subjects which employed empirical methods, basing knowledge on observation and evidence.

The study of the film industry, which is now an important part of film studies, is situated in a range of different disciplines and academic areas, including film history, the political and economic analysis of culture (for example, Marxist and ideological approaches) and an empirical analysis of the development of the film industry. Across these different approaches, similar questions are raised; how does the organization and structure of the film industry shape the types of films which are produced? Will films produced within a capitalist system inevitably reflect the capitalist ideology?

The study of the film industry has, though, also raised concerns that in the discussion of production, marketing and distribution, the film itself would be lost. In order to avoid this, theorists have attempted to create a balance between the textual analysis of specific films and an awareness of the system which produced them. This would include, at an empirical level, how the budget of a film will affect the way in which a film-maker can tell the story, and perhaps even the type of stories that can be told.

Industry and institution

Within this field of study the terms industry and institution, although often used interchangeably, also have specific meanings and connotations within methodologies. In addition to describing a particular type of organization, the selection of one term over another can indicate a particular approach to the analysis of film production. Film historians tend to examine the objective evidence about the film industry at a particular time and place: evidence based on research through primary sources. In contrast, the term institution carries with it wider meanings, once again showing how cultural studies has influenced film studies. In cultural studies the term institution refers to the influence that social, political and economic contexts have on the production and consumption of a media text. Inherent in the use of the term institution is the argument that these contexts will affect film style and content, making film an ideological practice. However, it is soon apparent that, in practice, there is an overlap in these methodologies – for example, film historians will argue that a particular film style is the result of cultural and economic factors.

Film history and the film industry

In order to gain a greater understanding of the relationship between the film text and the organizational structure which produces them, film studies has been particularly influenced by methodologies from history. The historical method refers to the method of using primary sources and other forms of evidence to write histories and to find explanations for particular events. In film studies, these explanations concern the history of film style and changing industry practice.

The influential film historian David Bordwell (2008) has defined the range of approaches which belong to the practice of film history and discussed its aims. The film historian is interested in asking questions about past production, exhibition and distribution practices. These questions focus on factual evidence: who produced this film and how many more like it were made? Where was this film shown and who saw it? Why weren't new technologies integrated within film production as soon as they were available? The answers to these questions have to be found through historical research, focusing on archives and primary sources. The aim of the film historian is to provide an accurate account of the historical (and contemporary) workings of the film industry, believing that this must be in place before any kind of evaluation or interpretive analysis can occur.

Film history encompasses a variety of areas. It includes biographical history of an individual's life within the context of their historical period; this may include star biographies but also studies of less well-known figures such as agents and producers. Technological history examines the processes and materials which are part of production and exhibition practices, including histories of the development of sound, colour and widescreen technologies. Aesthetic history – one of Bordwell's key areas of research – provides a record of the features of film style during a particular period and place, such as Hollywood during the 1930s. This objective, non-interpretive approach is also referred to as historical poetics and is in opposition to the evaluative and ideological readings which dominate other areas of film studies (see Chapter 7 for a discussion of the poetic approach in film studies). A further area of study in film history, that of the social, cultural and political history of film, overlaps with a number of other methodologies. For example, work on fan cultures in the UK during the 1940s uses historical, psychoanalytic and analytical approaches (see Stacey, 1994), while the recent development in 'geographical cultures' uses historical research into the history of film exhibition to discuss the relationship between audience and film (see Jancovich et al, 2003).

In the context of the specific business practices of the film industry, economic or industrial history has used primary research of studio archives to construct a greater understanding of how the film business operates, and how it affects film style and audience experience. Bordwell (2008) argues that this work is indispensable in the development of film studies as a discipline:

> Accurate description is indispensable for all historical research. Scholars have spent countless hours identifying films, collating versions, compiling filmographies, establishing timelines, and creating reference works that supply names, dates, and the like. The more sophisticated and long-lived a historical discipline is, the richer and more complete its battery of descriptive reference material will be.

The genius of the system: Film history and the Hollywood studio system

In *The Genius of the System: Hollywood Filmmaking in the Studio Era*, Thomas Schatz (1998) illustrates many of the key aims and methods of film history's approach to the film industry. Like much of the historical work in this area, the focus is on Hollywood during the studio system. The reason for the focus on this period of film history is fairly obvious: Hollywood had been – and is – the dominant global business in film production and distribution, and the studio system was singular in its explicit adoption of factory practices. Related to this, the seeming paradox of a highly structured system which also produced the 'golden age' of Hollywood cinema was of great interest to academics. Schatz's work is also typical in that it sets up the historical method in opposition to film theory – in this case, auteur theory – to demonstrate the inadequacy of theoretical approaches which are not based on historical fact.

As the title of his book makes clear, Schatz is arguing for recognition that the great films of Hollywood's golden age are a product of a particular system rather than of individual creativity and artistry. In doing this he is directly challenging the version of the history of film, which has been written by auteur theory critics, a history which, he claims, has done damage to an understanding of film history by stalling it in 'a prolonged stage of romanticism' (Schatz, 1998, p8). In the auteur history, the studio system had been a director's cinema, where the auteur's individual style was, in large part, a product of their antagonism towards the studio system. In this theory the studio system is characterized as 'the dehumanizing, formulaic, profit hungry machinery of Hollywood's studio-factories' (Schatz, 1998, p5). Shatz singles out Andrew Sarris's influential auteur study *The American Cinema* (1968) as an example of the type of approach which has reduced film history to the careers of a few dozen heroic directors who struggled against the oppression of the studio bosses. This romantic narrative had not just been provided by auteur critics, but was part of a wider context of autobiographical writing, interviews and critical studies which reinforced the oppositional structure of the studio system – that of the artist versus the system – with great films being produced despite rather than because of it.

The historical approach to the studio system was, in Schatz's words, an attempt to 'calculate the whole equation of pictures' (Schatz, 1998, p8). This was done through the analysis of a vast range of primary sources: industry documents which had been produced by the studio system in its need to keep strict control of accounting. These included memos, corporate correspondence, budgets, schedules, story conference notes, detailed production reports and censorship files. The analysis of this material is necessary to fulfil Schatz's aim of explaining how 'various social, industrial, technological, economic and aesthetic forces struck a delicate balance' (Schatz, 1998, p8). Rather than a cinema of auteurs, Schatz argues that it is institutional forces which were responsible for the film style developed during this period. Directors were one part of the studio style, which was a coalescence of visual style, story, genre and stars, rather than the creators of an individual expression. There were, though, Schatz acknowledges, certain directors who had greater freedom within the system, such as John Ford, Alfred Hitchcock, Howard

141

Hawks and Frank Capra. Their greater freedom was a result of a combination of these particular directors' 'style and authority'. The authority or power to make the films they chose tended to be based on their role as producers rather than directors, and their ability to develop a recognizable style was a function of commercial success; it made economic sense for the studios to develop a popular style. In this account, the development of a director's signature style is part of the model of the system. This model meant that individual studios conformed to an overarching film style of genre film-making and classic narrative, but differentiated themselves by marketing through genre and stars. Therefore, the Warner Bros studio was associated with urban genres such as the gangster film and thriller, and with stars linked to that style such as James Cagney and Edward G. Robinson.

Schatz's account of the studio era has been criticized for romanticizing the idea of the 'genius' of the studio system, just as auteur theorists have been accused of distorting film history through their emphasis on individual contributions. This historical approach does, though, raise issues to be addressed by auteur critics, and it has influenced the way in which film studies understands the nature of auteur theory. Auteur theory has been expanded to include stars, producers and studios as the creators of meaning in a film, rather than being rejected entirely.

Political economics of culture

In contrast to the historical approach to the film industry, which focuses on the detail of specific production processes, the political economic approach is more interested in the relationship between popular cultural forms (popular music, TV, films, etc.) and the audience. In some ways this approach shares similarities with the mass culture critics of the 1930s. Mass culture critics, following the ideas of the Frankfurt School during the 1930s, developed the concept of the 'culture industry'. They argued that the institutions which produce culture, such as Hollywood, are part of an industry, an ideological system which reinforces capitalist values. More problematic for proponents of political economic theory was the mass culture idea that resistance to the ideological project could be found through avant-garde works of high culture. Mass culture critics argued that high art was isolated from the commercialized nature of popular culture rather than recognizing it as a form of culture which serves the tastes and interests of dominant groups. This rejection of some of the elitist analysis of the mass culture theorists made a political and economic analysis of the film industry more attractive. This approach combined Marxist analysis with a historical approach in order to explain the interaction between artists, industries and audiences, seeing this relationship as an interactive and, at times, contradictory one, rather than one based purely on ideological practices.

The work of Nicholas Garnham has been influential across the humanities and social sciences, as well as in public cultural policy discussions in examining the way in which cultural institutions operate. In *Capitalism and Communication* (Garnham, 1990), he uses the economics of the US film industry to exemplify the way in which cultural production is shaped by its economic context. In this analysis, unlike the ideological model of mass culture theorists, Garnham argues that the process is driven by the contradictory need for the film industry to reach a diverse range of audiences, but also to work in a conventional, consistent style to maximize profits, the latter working against the needs of the former.

Garnham identifies three distinctive features of the culture industry which are directly applicable to Hollywood film production. The industry is capital intensive; the use of the latest technology means that it is a very expensive industry to enter; this, in turn, limits diversity. Film studios are complex structures based on hierarchical systems and power structures, the aim of which is to maximize efficiency and profit. Hollywood shares these characteristics with many other industries; but institutions which produce culture also have specific difficulties associated with them which other forms of production do not. Culture is not a necessity, and people's ability to pay for films will fluctuate, as will the amount of time they have available for film viewing – whether due to work or family commitments. While Hollywood can be fairly confident that it produces a popular product, it is also difficult – despite the use of focus groups and audience research – to predict which particular film will do well and which will flop at the box office. To guard against failure, studios have to try to attract mass audiences with blockbuster films, but also to provide films which appeal to a range of diverse audiences in case the blockbuster fails.

This analysis of the film industry, where success is reliant on matching the right film to the right audience, can help to explain how the power in the industry has shifted from production to distribution, a characteristic feature of the 'New' or 'post-classical' Hollywood. The political economic analysis of the film industry challenges some assumptions that have been made about Hollywood as an industry. Rather than the stereotypical concept of Hollywood films as a homogeneous product appealing to an undifferentiated mass, this analysis shows how Hollywood has exploited diversity to survive, aiming films at a range of niche audiences, including, at different times, the youth market, audiences for art and independent cinema, and African-American audiences. This range of films produced for a range of audiences is the result, it is argued, of the increased fragmentation of the Hollywood film industry. The post-studio system model of multiple companies within a single conglomerate allows for the development of different film styles and practices.

Global conglomerates and the high-concept film

The analysis of film style as the product of its industrial context is exemplified in Schatz's work on the high concept film. In his essay 'The New Hollywood' (1993), he demonstrates how the high-concept film emerged as the successor to the Hollywood blockbuster and was a product of the conglomerate structure which was driven by the need to address a global audience. This analysis suggests that the film industry is concerned not so much with films themselves, but with ensuring that those films are shown and seen – because Hollywood's dominance in film lies in its control of exhibition and distribution. Maltby (1998) describes the changes in the industry in the following terms:

> movie production can be seen as the creation of entertainment software that can be viewed through several different windows and transported to several different platforms maintained by other divisions of tightly diversified media corporations . . . less than 20% of total film revenues come from domestic box office.

The different ways in which films are now received have had a symbiotic relationship with changes in the industry; the different 'delivery systems' of video, cable, satellite, digital and the internet allow much wider distribution of films than traditional cinema exhibition, creating a truly global audience.

The need to address a global audience in order to survive has led to changes in film style, with the high-concept film seen as a result of the need to address the widest range of cultures, rather than an artistically driven form. 'High concept' is an academic model rather than an industry one and it refers to a list of characteristics which are the result of a series of economic determinants. These include the shift to one-film deals from assembly-line production of the studio system, which has meant more money going into the making of fewer films. This, in turn, means that the films that are produced need to return large profits, and therefore have to appeal to a global audience. It is in addressing this question – how to produce a film which appeals to a global audience of millions – that the conventions of the high-concept film have been developed. The high-concept film is post-generic hybrid film-making based on simplified character and narrative; it uses styles which are recognizable from other popular forms such as music video, TV and advertising, and these are easily used for marketing purposes. High-concept films tend to rely on special effects to create exaggerated and exciting moments which do not rely on nuances of character and emotion. The logical extreme of the high-concept film is that the film itself becomes merely an advert for all the merchandizing and marketing around it.

Criticisms of institutional analysis

The institutional analysis approach has been accused of 'economic determinism', of seeing films as simply a reflection of the industry which produced them, removing any sense of the creative individuals working within the industry. In attempting to correct the apparent inaccuracies of auteur theory in its focus on the individual, institutional analysis – whether historical or ideological – was considered to have gone too far in the opposite direction. Ideological analysis assumes that films reflect dominant ideology because it is a capitalist institution which produces them. It then sets out to show how this is achieved, rather than questioning whether this is the case. In doing so, the conception of the film industry as a homogeneous entity ignores the way in which some films seem to explicitly challenge the dominant system and the variety of beliefs held by individual workers within the industry. Richard Dyer (1998, p9) points to the difficulty of getting the right balance between the study of producers and the study of film texts:

> the aesthetic and the cultural cannot stand in opposition. The aesthetic dimension of a film never exists apart from how it is conceptualized, how it is socially practised, how it is received; it never exists floating free of historical and social particularity. Equally the cultural study of film must always recognize that it is studying film.

New technology, industry and the challenges for film studies

Recent developments in the economic and historical analysis of the film industry have been to look at the effects of new technology on the organizational systems of the industry and the film style produced. This work includes arguments of economic determinism – for example, in the analysis of 3D film as a response to the illegal downloads which threaten Hollywood dominance and profitability – but also an aesthetic approach which analyses the changing conventions of film style in relation to new digital technology. Both of these areas raise questions about traditional definitions of what film is and how the audience consumes it.

In film studies, these significant changes in the production, distribution and exhibition of films created by global corporatization and developments in technology were seen to coincide with crises in the discipline itself. The status of film as an art form was seen as under threat from an increasingly corporatized culture which could just as easily produce cars as film. In parallel with this was the challenge posed to film's status as the most popular cultural form of the twentieth century by the new media forms of the twenty-first century. The advent of digitization and computer-generated imagery meant that the fundamental identity of film as a material form which was capable of capturing the physical, recognizable world and reflecting it back to an audience was also in doubt. Film theorists have debated the effect of these changes, with some arguing that these developments represent a significant transformation in film style and exhibition, while others contend that the film experience has remained fundamentally the same.

One of the key areas of discussion has been over theories of realism and film, which have been fundamental to film studies as a discipline since the 1950s. In this period, the extremely influential French critic André Bazin proposed that film's status as an art form lay in its affinity for realism – that it is indexical (see Chapter 6 for further discussion of Bazin and realism in film). One theorist of new media, Len Manovich, claims that the advent of digitization has meant that film no longer has this direct relationship with the physical world. To demonstrate this he points to the nature of digital film-making, where it is no longer necessary to film a physical reality, but instead 'film-like' scenes can be generated directly on a computer with 3D animation. In addition to this, while live action footage was left intact in traditional film-making, it is now merely the raw material for 'further compositing, animating and morphing' (Manovich, 2010, p249). This means that the production process itself has been transformed, with post-production stages now likely to be ten times as long as the production itself. Manovich gives the example of the production process for *Star Wars Episode 1 – The Phantom Menace* (1999), where traditional filming took 65 days but post-production took two years due to the large percentage (95 per cent) of the shots in the film that were constructed on a computer (Manovich, 2010, p250).

In contrast to this view, there is a growing debate about the usefulness of theories of cinematic realism itself. These range from questioning whether cinema has ever been simply an indexical and realist form, to whether digital photography is still indexical, to different interpretations of the way in which film is realist. This last aspect has been influenced by theories of 'affect' in film: the idea that the experience of watching a film, particularly its central characteristic of motion, creates a specific affect for the audience, which is real – it doesn't rely on the realist representation of an image. This would suggest that digital cinema is still a realist cinema. Tom Gunning, a historian of film aesthetics, argues that the whole basis of cinema and realism needs to be questioned, that it has always been a flawed concept. In his analysis of the use of digital animation in film-making, he argues that:

> While flaunting the rules of physical resemblance, such animation need not remain totally divorced from any reference to our lived world . . . the cartoon body can reveal primal phenomenological relations we have to our physical existence, our sense of grasping, stretching, exulting. (Gunning, 2010, p266)

At the same time that questions of the effect of the changing material nature of film were being posed, it was also apparent that new ways of viewing films would also have to be integrated withn film studies' ideas about audiences. In an influential essay on this subject provocatively entitled 'The end of cinema: Multimedia and technological change', Anne Friedberg (2010) argues that the unique experience of watching films on a large screen in a darkened auditorium, having made a specific decision about what to watch, has largely been replaced by viewing on home cinema systems and computer screens (to which could now be added smart phones and tablets). This viewing is just one among the many viewing opportunities available at any one time; it is no longer the absorbing, even overwhelming experience that it once was. If this is the case, then it clearly has major implications for theories of the audience in film studies. Having moved away from the concept of the single homogeneous viewer to the idea of diverse audiences, new forms of exhibition seem to challenge the fundamental relationship between spectator and film.

Not all theorists agree with this analysis, though, pointing to the way in which figures for cinema attendance have remained steady, even rising around the world, despite the diverse ways of watching films and the greatly improved quality of the home viewing experience. The sustained popularity of cinema-going indicates that going to a movie is not just about watching a film, which

147

in turn suggests other areas of enquiry into the relationship between audience and film. In his overview of recent developments in the theoretical aspects of film studies as a discipline, Marc Furstenau (2010) is optimistic about the future of film studies, arguing that these dramatic changes in the nature of cinema will reinvigorate the discipline, providing a range of challenging new questions to address: 'The arguments about the present and future status of film have enlivened the discipline, and have generated significant debates about the present and future status of film theory.'

Summary

- The study of the industrial context of film had been neglected by film studies due to the emphasis on film as an art form.
- The historical analysis of the film industry is often used to challenge film theory.
- The analysis of institutions tends to see a direct link between the organization of the institution and the style of films produced.
- The study of the industry has, at times, been accused of seeing the industry and its product as homogeneous, rather than acknowledging the diversity of film style, subjects and makers.

References and further reading

Bordwell, D. (2008) *Doing Film History*, September, http://www.davidbordwell.net/essays/doing.php, accessed 6 April 2012

Dyer, R. (1998) 'Introduction to film studies', in P. C. J. Hill (ed) *The Oxford Guide to Film Studies*, Oxford University Press, Oxford

Friedberg, A. (2010) 'The end of cinema: Multimedia and technological change', in M. Furstenau (ed) *The Film Theory Reader*, Routledge, London, pp270–281

Furstenau, M. (2010) 'Introduction', in M. Furstenau (ed) *The Film Theory Reader*, Routledge, London, pp1–20

Garnham, N. (1990) *Capitalism and Communication: Global Culture and the Politics of Information*, Sage, London

Gunning, T. (2010) 'Moving away from the index', in M. Furstenau (ed) *The Film Theory Reader*, Routledge, London, pp255–269

Jancovich, M., Faire, L. with Stubbings, S. (2003) *The Place of the Audience: Cultural Geographies of Film Consumption*, British Film Institute, London

Maltby, R. (1998) 'Nobody knows everything', in S. Neale (ed) *Contemporary Hollywood Cinema: Post Classical Historiographies and Consolidated Entertainment*, Routledge, London, pp21–23

Manovich, L. (2010) 'Digital cinema and the history of a moving image', in M. Furstenau (ed) *The Film Theory Reader*, Routledge, London, pp245–254

Sarris, A. (1968) *The American Cinema: Directors and Directions, 1929–1968*, Da Capo Press, New York, NY

Schatz, T. (1993) 'The New Hollywood', in J. Collins, H. Radner and A. Preacher (eds) *Film Theory Goes to the Movies*, Routledge, London, pp8–36

— (1998) *The Genius of the System: Hollywood Filmmaking in the Studio Era*, Faber and Faber, London

Stacey, J. (1994) *Star Gazing: Hollywood Cinema and Female Spectatorship*, Routledge, London

In addition to academic studies of the film industry there are many informative and entertaining books by people who work in it. One of the most famous is *Adventures in the Screen Trade* (Macdonald, 1984) by the successful Hollywood scriptwriter William Goldman, which provides an insight into his creative process and the problems he faced in working in the 'system'. The autobiography of Joe Eszterhaus (at one point the highest-paid scriptwriter in Hollywood), *Hollywood Animal* (Random House, 2004), provides a more recent – and controversial – account of living and working in Hollywood.

The role of the producer is explored in a range of histories and autobiographies. These include Stephen Bach's *Final Cut: Art, Money and Ego in the Making of 'Heaven's Gate', the Film that Sank United Artists* (Newmarket, 1999); Julia Phillips's *You'll Never Eat Lunch in This Town Again* (Faber and Faber, 2002), which details her life as an independent film producer and drug addict in Hollywood during the 1970s and 1980s; and Art Linson's *What Just Happened? Bitter Hollywood Tales from the Front Line* (Bloomsbury, 2003).

The journalist Peter Biskind has written several popular histories of specific periods in American cinema: *Easy Riders, Raging Bulls: How the Sex-Drugs-and-Rock 'n' Roll Generation Changed Hollywood* (Bloomsbury, 1999) is an account of the emergence of the 'New Hollywood' of the 1960s and 1970s, and is based on interviews with many of the key actors, writers and directors of the period.

Index